OLD AGE POVERTY IN GREENWICH VILLAGE

Greenwich House Series No. 6

Old Age Poverty in Greenwich Village

A NEIGHBORHOOD STUDY

BY

MABEL LOUISE NASSAU

Introduction by

HENRY R. SEAGER
Professor of Political Economy, Columbia University

NEW YORK CHICAGO TORONTO

Fleming H. Revell Company

LONDON AND EDINBURGH

New York: 158 Fifth Avenue
Chicago: 125 N. Wabash Ave.
Toronto: 25 Richmond St., W.
London: 21 Paternoster Square
Edinburgh: 100 Princes Street

INTRODUCTION

OLD age poverty is a problem of growing seriousness in the United States. Providing for the aged members of a family in rural communities involves little or no burden, because on the farm or in the village there is always work that such persons may do, and the item of rent is negligible. This is far from the case in cities. As years go by, employers are more and more reluctant to take on employees who are past middle life. Moreover, the requirements of modern industry have become so exacting that older people are at an increasing disadvantage in competition with those who have the greater quickness and adaptability of youth. "Grown old at forty" means less that modern industry so saps the vitality of the worker that he must be discarded at that age than that modern methods are better served by younger persons. This unfavorable industrial situation is paralleled by the greatly increased expense in cities of maintaining an added member of a family in idleness. Old people have thus come to be a burden upon the family to which they belong. That this burden is usually willingly borne should not blind us to the fact that it adds not a little to the difficulties of the normal wage-earning family in connection with meeting the rising expenses of living.

The above facts are familiar to social students, but it remained for Miss Nassau to bring together convincing illustrations of them for our own city of New York. Her study embraces one hundred of the aged neighbors whom she learned to know as a resident of Greenwich House. Greenwich Village is neither better nor worse than the other districts of New York in which wage-earners predominate. If Miss Nassau's description is true to the facts for this part of New York, it may be accepted as substantially true to the facts for the city at large.

Although her one hundred aged persons were selected at random, great care was taken to include none who were not obviously representative of large groups. By classifying her examples into six groups, the author succeeds in indicating how varied is the problem.

Many of these aged persons are not dependent on charity, or likely to become so. Through their own industry, through contributions of their families, or through pensions, they are freed from material anxieties. It is striking, however, that the great majority of these Greenwich House neighbors either already feel the pinch of poverty, or else are haunted by the fear that before long they may be brought to want. That so many lives should be embittered by fear of dependency culminating in life " on the Island " and the pauper's grave is a serious reflection on our civilization.

Miss Naussau's study is not an argument for any particular plan of caring for the aged poor. At the same time, her discussion of the various plans that have been proposed and of their merits and demerits from the point of view of the evidence which she has collected, supplies convincing proof of the need of some broad, constructive policy.

Combining the interest and pathos of biography with the objectivity of a social investigation, Miss Nassau's book is to be commended to the attention of all those desirous of knowing the conditions under which one large class of people lives in New York, and of contributing toward the amelioration of those conditions.

HENRY R. SEAGER.

COLUMBIA UNIVERSITY,
May 14, 1915.

CONTENTS

PREFACE

THE following studies were made while in residence at Greenwich House Settlement during the winter of 1913-14, under the direction of Professor Henry R. Seager.

The purpose of the study was to find out, through a small intensive study of individuals, how well the aged poor are provided for, by their own efforts, by their families and by existing charitable agencies, and to see what further provision is needed.

One hundred people over sixty years of age, living in the area known as Greenwich Village (between Fourteenth and Canal Streets and lower Fifth Avenue and West Broadway to the Hudson River), near or under the actual poverty line, were selected for special inquiry and for as accurate delineation as possible.

Obviously one hundred people do not afford a basis for statistics or for sweeping general observations, but from such a group individuals can be chosen that are typical of larger groups. The classification of groups in Chapters II.-VII. are surely broad enough to include a large number of people, and the carefully selected types described in them and in the succeeding chapters are, I am convinced, normal and representative.

Since it seems fair to believe that the representative types of this study are representative of the old people in the city at large, I have put forth the conclusions which I have drawn from them with a good deal of confidence.

With the genuine desire to be fair, "unworthy" as well as "worthy" illustrations are given, though probably the people described, as a whole represent, in intelligence and morals, a higher standard than might be found in some other more crowded districts, or in districts less well supplied with churches and settlements, or in a regular house-to-house canvass.

A few of the people interviewed were met on the street, or suggested by neighbors, but most of the names of those called upon were given by organizations. Appeals for lists of names were made in person to the churches of all denominations in the district (twelve churches were asked to co-operate), to the settlements, to the A. I. C. P. and to the C. O. S., to a day nursery, to a milk station, to one of the district visiting nurses, to a hospital and to a dispensary, to three men's hotels, to St. Andrew's coffee-stand, to the Salvation Army, etc. The majority responded helpfully, though some were able to give only two to five names, while others contributed ten to twenty names. Many names were unavailable because out of the district limits, or under the age desired, or because the people themselves were unwilling to give information, or were out working when called upon, or had changed addresses.

At first I did not reveal the real purpose of the investigation, but made a "friendly visit." But afterward I was advised to do so, because, as an experienced church visitor said, "The old people are asking what you are 'after'; they guess you are 'up to something.'" When I did state my purpose, nearly all were willing to help by answering questions, sometimes with a desire to help the cause, sometimes (not understanding the matter at all clearly) with the hope of immediate personal gain.

Unfortunately a number of women, in upper and lower Greenwich Village, had been interviewed some time before by someone "who asked some of the same questions as you, but she was from Washington." And, it was explained further, "she had big sealed papers and she was going to send all the answers back to Washington, and she asked for twenty-five cents from me and from Mrs. —— and Mrs. —— for postage, and we never heard anything from her again." This person, evidently a "fake," must have made quite a little sum for herself, and it needed patient explanations to show the difference of the investigation I was conducting.

Some people, with no faith whatever in any definite results, gave information as a personal kindness. A plan to start a "grandmothers' club" had to be given up, as the women were mostly too busy working, or else too infirm to come to the settlement. Some people were visited only once, others several times, and the information gained in interviews was eked out by those giving the lists. Some of the organizations allowed their names to be used as introductions, but sometimes names were given with the distinct understanding that the visits were to appear as casual. Some organizations, while showing sympathy with the investigation, refused to give names, or were unable to give names. Thus, on the whole, interest and kindness were shown everywhere by organizations and by the people themselves.

I

GENERAL ASPECTS OF THE PROBLEM

ONE of the first impressions I received in starting out on this investigation was, that the aged are not a problem by themselves. The aged cannot be considered separately, for their destinies are interwoven inextricably with those of their families, and with that of society as a whole.

In calling upon the aged member of the family, the whole family history was unrolled;—what affected the aged, affected the middle-aged, and the children, so that the problem assumed far wider and deeper significance than I was prepared to expect.

The whole situation seems very little understood by people in comfortable circumstances. Only a few special students of economics, philanthropists and social workers appreciate its seriousness, and what an exceedingly small proportion of society they compose!

Important books have been written on the subjects of social insurance and old age pensions. Among them, in order of the date of their publication, are: 1, "Pauperism and the Endowment of Old Age," by Charles Booth (1892); 2, "State Insurance," by Frank W. Lewis (1909); 3, "Social Insurance," by Henry R. Seager (1910); 4, "Workingmen's Insurance in Europe," by Frankel and Dawson (1910); 5, "Old-Age Dependency in the United States," by L. W. Squier (1912); 6, "Social Insurance," by I. M. Rubinow (1913).

On page 239 of his book L. W. Squier says: "That the problem is present; that it is widespread; that it deeply concerns our national happiness and prosperity; that its demands are insistent, and that the attempt at its permanent solution must be nation-, perhaps world-wide, cannot be doubted by an intelligent observer of economic conditions to-day"; and I. M. Rubinow, in his chapter on "The Old Man's Problem in Modern Industry," says (pp. 301 and 302):

"Unfortunately these blessings of civilization, like most other blessings for that matter, have not benefited all classes of society—not in the same degree, anyway. For side by side with the achievements of old age in arts, literature, business, professions, science and statesmanship, modern civilization on its industrial side has created the very grave problem of superannuation—the problem of the jobless, helpless, incomeless, and propertyless old man of fifty." Later (p. 304) he says: "Second, the economic conditions of the wage-contract accentuate the economic disability of old age. Under normal physiological conditions, old age, unless preceded by a definite chronic ailment, should lead to a gradual failing of the productive process. As the medieval independent worker became old, he worked less and produced less, but he went on working as long as he could produce something. For an agricultural community, the usefulness of an old man or woman does not cease until actual senility is established, and actual senility is a comparatively rare phenomenon. But under a wage system, the condition is altogether different."

These quotations show the trend of scientific thought, and the books mentioned and others give full information concerning the measures that are being taken abroad and in America to solve the problem on the legislative side.

In the following pages I have attempted to supplement these scientific treatises by giving my concrete observations, gained in personal contact with the people discussed, describing their conditions as I found them.

It is always very difficult for a member of one social group to understand thoroughly the conditions affecting a member of a different group. We may have approximate experiences, but never very similar ones. The best we can do is to enter, as far as possible, through imagination and intuition, and by a process of cumulative study and sympathetic inquiry, the lives of many individuals in another group, and thus enter into a kind of other-group consciousness—to think and feel, as it were, in terms of those whom we are trying to comprehend. In this spirit of trying to see the individual as an individual, and yet in the proper relation to his heritage and environment, the following studies are given. Until the poor are considered not only economically but individually, with all their personal equations taken into account, we cannot solve their problems, any more than we can solve their problems by regarding them merely as individuals without taking into account their economic relations.

This report is, then, largely a description of individuals, supplemented by a few cautious generalizations.

After interviewing a number of people, I decided to divide the aged persons studied for better understanding into six groups, according to their source of maintenance, giving, under each group, descriptions of typical people. This was rather difficult, because each person was very distinct and, in a way, each seemed unique. Still, there was enough similarity in their present conditions, if not in their histories, to make them fit into such a simple classification. Also, it was difficult to decide just which "cases" illustrated each group or chapter best—for some really illustrate several. The classification is thus not rigid, but it has the advantage of giving a few distinct pictures and contrasts, and of putting general facts and actual people into close juxtaposition.

As no statistics compiled from one hundred people would justify elaborate statistical analysis, statistical tables are introduced merely to show that the one hundred interviewed were a fairly varied group.

Here are a few general statistics:

Sex

Women	65
Men	35
	100

Ages

(Women)

60-64	18
65-69	13
70-79	21
80	4
?	9
	65

(Men)

60-64	15
65-69	11
70-79	8
80	1
	35

Nationalities

Women		Men
25	Irish	10
18	American	13
3	Colored	
4	English	
4	German	3
3	Italian	6
2	Scotch	2
1	French	
1	Canadian	
1	Swiss	
3	Unknown	1
65		35

Condition

Women—54 widows; 9 single; 2 separated.

Men—9 widowers; 3 single; 2 separated or divorced; 21 married.

I neglected to ask twenty-one women and eight men if they had savings, but of the rest five women and five men had savings—that is, ten out of seventy-one had savings. The savings of the five women were partly left to them by someone else, and, except in one case, could not last long. Of the five men, two were bachelors and could thus save fairly easily; one had savings sufficient for one year only, and another's savings were fast diminishing. So that the savings counted for little. The reason I neglected to ask the twenty-nine people if they had savings was, usually, that they so obviously had nothing.

Almost none of the people interviewed had had early industrial training. I neglected to ask twenty-five of the women if they had had special training, but of the forty I did ask, only three were trained—of those one for dressmaking, one for tailoring and one for millinery. Of the men eleven were not asked, but of the twenty-four asked, six were trained—two in Germany, one as a shoemaker and one as a builder; one in Scotland as a shoemaker, one in Italy as a blacksmith, and two in New York, one as a bricklayer and one as a carriage-builder. Lists of occupations are given in each of the six groups.

Women were engaged almost entirely in the traditional women's occupations—sewing, dressmaking, washing, scrubbing, domestic service and janitress work, with a few in factories and stores. The work, as a whole, was very unskilled work, with a few exceptions. Probably in another generation there will be more variety in women's work. Most of the men were also unskilled workers, though a few worked in factories and had trades, such as painter, mason, carpenter, shoemaker, bricklayer, printer, baker. Then there were a number of longshoremen and truckmen, and a number had little street stands, or helped their sons in stores.

There are certain generalizations which might be made about widows and widowers, couples, and single men and women, but one hundred people seem scarcely a safe basis for generalizations, especially as this study aims to be a study of individuals in relation to the general problem.

There is, however, one common quality found, not only in each group, but in almost all persons interviewed, and that was economic fear. Fear was shown by nearly all of the self-supporting persons, that their ability to work might not last much longer. Fear was shown by those dependent on their families, that the relative who was the source of support might lose his or her job, or might marry and with other demands be unable to help. Fear was shown by those dependent (wholly or partly) on charity, that they would not receive sufficient or continuous help.

The fear of being forced into some institution was widespread and intense. Then there was the fear of illness. Of course the fear of illness is not confined to the poor or aged, but it is most serious for the poor, because they literally cannot afford to be sick. It is one thing to be ill, with the care and comforts which money can buy, added to the care and consideration that can be given by relatives who have leisure; but it is another matter to be ill when almost penniless, and when relatives are already overburdened with work. The combination of being old and poor and ill is tragic!

By this I do not mean to imply that I found all the people I interviewed unhappy. Many were cheerful; some because of fine character, and some because they were so stupid or so selfish that they did not realize, or did not care, that they were a burden to their families or to society. On the whole, however, I was impressed by the worthiness of most of the people I met, by their simple virtues of unselfishness, cheerfulness and courage, and by the dignity with which they bore their hardships.

II

AGED PEOPLE WHO ARE SELF-SUPPORTING

THIS group contains twenty-seven persons. Their occupations are as follows:

Nine widows:

One lives on savings.
One lives on savings and takes lodgers.
One dressmaker.
One does sewing.
One takes child as boarder and sells newspapers.
One does office scrubbing.
One does day's work out and washing at home.
Two in domestic service.

One single woman:

Has two furnished-room houses.

Ten couples:

(For couples the history of the man is given.)

Two live on savings.
One clerk.
Two janitors with wives' assistance.
One truckman.
One has street candy and peanut stand.
One in store, but is about to lose job.
Two help sons in stores.

Three widowers:

One works on docks.
One bricklayer.
One night-watchman.

Two single men:

One janitor with odd carpentry jobs.
One has savings.

Two separated or divorced men:

One umbrella-mender
One has newsstand.

Four people belonging to this group are described in the chapter, "Difficulties of Saving for Old Age"; one widow (No. 93), one couple (No. 39), one widower (No. 56), and one single man (No. 62).

The following descriptions are given here as the best illustrations of this group: four widows, the one single woman, two couples, one widower and the two separated or divorced men.

No. 6—Mrs. C.

Mrs. C. is sixty-two years old, and (now that her varicose veins have grown so bad that she can't work) has a little top-floor back room in a furnished-room house, though until recently she received $5.00 a week in domestic service. She was a servant before she married, so she naturally turned to that after her husband died sixteen years ago. He was a mechanical engineer, and died on a trip to Japan, leaving no savings. Mrs. C. has had to stop work before because of illness, and each time her savings have been broken into. This time they are nearly gone, and the visiting nurse told me she probably can never work out again, though she thinks she can begin work again soon. The clergyman of her church thinks she ought to go into a Home, but she refuses to do that. She is independent and cheerful, and doesn't want charity. She is cooking on the oil stove that heats her room, just enough to keep her alive, and has perfect faith that she can get a good position again just as soon as she can stand on her feet and hobble around.

Her children are dead, and she has no one to help her. She says she spends $3.50 a week, for room, heating, food, etc.

No. 1—Mrs. B.

Mrs. B. I met selling papers on the street. She is sixty-eight years old and shuffles along painfully, with ragged shoes. Occasionally she falls down with attacks of dizziness, but she manages to make about $2.00 a week from the papers.

I went home with her and found her pretty young granddaughter of seventeen years sick in bed. This granddaughter lives with Mrs. B. because her mother drinks and is immoral, and the girl feels she can't live in such a home, though apparently she and her mother are on speaking terms, and work in the same horse-radish factory nearby.

With Mrs. B.'s $2.00 a week, $10.00 a month paid for the board of a child (to whom Mrs. B. gives devotion but not very competent care) and the granddaughter's wages, the family budget covers usual expenses. But the granddaughter has been operated upon for appendicitis and now is sick again. At my suggestion the C. O. S. was asked to help with the rent, and the request was granted, but of course the C. O. S. can't keep on paying their rent.

The granddaughter feels the responsibility of aiding in her grandmother's support, and the grandmother feels the need of working just as long as she can drag around, and dreads the idea of being dependent on her delicate granddaughter.

Mrs. B.'s second husband died twenty years ago and left no savings. She took in washing, took children to board and sold newspapers. She used to make about $6.00 a week.

They have three rooms, of which one is light, in a disreputable street, and the rooms are dirty, but that is not surprising, as the girl stands all day at her factory work, and Mrs. B. exhausts her strength selling the papers and doing the necessary cooking.

The immoral mother keeps a young son with her. One wishes he could take refuge with the grandmother too, but until he can work, who would support him?

And yet with it all,—her fear and her growing weakness,—Mrs. B. keeps a brave, sweet and even cheerful outlook on life!

No. 48—Mrs. W.

Mrs. W. is a widow, an office scrubwoman. She is sixty-two, Irish, but has lived in New York forty-nine years. Before she married she was a domestic servant, so after her husband's death, thirty years ago (he was a street laborer), she went out washing and ironing, which gave her about $7.00 to $8.00 a week. Now she does office cleaning at $6.00 a week. She had three daughters who died; one who worked in a flower factory died quite recently. She lives alone except for a lodger to whom she rents a room for $1.50 a week, which reduces her rent of $13.00 a month, and leaves her enough for food, heat, clothing and some carfare. She says she walks as much as she can to save carfare, but the four trips a day—the office cleaning is done in two sessions—make too much walking.

She says she has no savings; probably the daughter's illness and the need of extra coal during an unusually severe winter took her savings.

Her lodger may leave, or her rheumatism may grow so much worse that she can't work, so her future isn't very secure!

No. 20—Mrs. H.

Mrs. H. is an Irish Catholic, sixty years old. She came to the United States when six years old, and had a convent training till she was fourteen years old. She then worked in a shirtwaist factory till she married. Her husband died fifteen years ago, leaving nothing but burial insurance. Her son left her some savings. She has a sister and two nieces, but they can't help her, and she lives alone with two lodgers, whose payments cover the rent and leave a little over. As she can't find work at present she lives on that "little over" and the savings. She must have difficulty getting on, and I fancy the savings are not enough to last much longer, as she is gloomy and pessimistic and worried about the future.

No. 11—Miss D.

Miss D. is a shrewd, energetic Irish spinster of seventy-five, still fairly well and strong. She was at one time a tailoress, but has had for years two furnished-room houses, paying the amazing rent of $1,600 for them, i.e. for both. There are twenty-one rooms, which she rents for $1.75 to $4.00 a week. She says that lately she just clears enough to live on, and she has a great deal of work, as she keeps the rooms in order herself. She says she has "lent relatives money," and that "they will have to take care of me when I can't work longer!" Aside from this rather unbusinesslike arrangement, she seems an example of a rather unusually intelligent woman of her class and she certainly is unusually strong physically. She isn't a fair example of what most women of her age can do. Of course, it remains to be seen how well these relatives will reward her. Single women are especially apt to be preyed upon by relatives, and when they have savings they rarely take proper care of them.

No. 5—Mr. B.

Mr. B. is a native American, sixty-three years old. He and his wife are still well and strong enough to work. They do janitor work for four houses, receiving four rooms, coal and gas free and $12.00 a month pay, which is just enough for food. Probably tips help out. He used to be a driver and a porter, averaged $16.00 a week, but they had thirteen children to provide for, and of the six left none can now help them. They have no savings and no insurance. I didn't see Mr. B., but Mrs. B. said they always wanted to be independent, and "when we can't care for ourselves we'll go to the poorhouse." It is easy enough for her to say that now when they can both work, and such a contingency seems impossible, but to the observer who thinks of old age and incapacity not far off, such reliance upon a capital of physical strength seems rather desperate. The woman made the speech in a belligerent tone, not as if she and her husband would ever go to the poorhouse with any willingness.

The following case illustrates a transitional stage which is typical probably of what will happen later with others described as self-supporting at present, but with the imminent possibility of being obliged to give up work.

No. 67—Mr. D. Z.

Mr. D. Z., over sixty, was introduced to me by some neighbors, who took me to call on him, evidently hoping I could help him in some way, and interpreted for me. He was born in Italy and has been in New York fourteen years, but never took out naturalization papers. It was probably a big mistake for him to leave Italy, as he had a position as a government forester there. At first he did brass work in a factory here, but now he is only a clerk in a candy store, receiving $4.50 to $5.00 a week, and even this job he is to lose soon. He can't speak English and seemed stupid and glum, so probably his employer can't be blamed for dismissing him, as he would not attract trade. His wife is in a hospital with tuberculosis. He lives alone. He has two sons, but apparently they can't help much, and the two Italian girls who interpreted seemed to think outside aid would be needed.

No. 57—Mr. B.

Mr. B. is one of my absolutely unauthenticated cases, but his story was interesting, and plausible enough. I met him on the street. He said he was seventy-two and was born in Scotland, but came to America when thirty years old and took out naturalization papers. He had learned shoemaking from his father, and followed that trade until his wife made him become a weaver because she was one. He didn't like being a weaver, and wasn't successful, and after her death went back to shoemaking —evidently with general relief, as he said she was so very difficult he never wished to marry again. But finally he had to give up shoemaking, and now he is a night-watchman at a men's hotel kept by a very stingy woman, who pays him only 35 cents a night in addition to a bed in the daytime. Out of that 35 cents he has to get his meals. He said, "I'll work till I have to go into an institution," and apparently was not alarmed, especially, at that prospect, because he is at present so uncomfortable. He has no relatives in this country, and at seventy-two he cannot expect to live so many more years. A small amount would enable such a man to live in independence and comfort at a Mills Hotel.

No. 52—Mr. A.

Mr. A.'s career must be a fairly typical one. He has a newsstand on Hudson Street, and is independent and cheerful in spite of his wooden leg. I had no one to authenticate his story, but it seemed probable. He was born in New Jersey sixty-three years ago, and worked on a farm, then he was a mason, and in an accident lost a leg. He worked in a restaurant, and finally settled at the newsstand. He said he took in about $1.00 a day. He was separated or divorced, probably the former, as poor people are rarely divorced. He has three children, but said, "They can't help me, and anyway I wouldn't want to depend on my children."

Aside from his lameness he is well. He has a "furnished room" somewhere, and must get on well on $7.00 a week just for himself, and be able to save something.

I met one or two other old men with little stands and felt as if that were quite an appropriate and pleasant mode of livelihood for men incapacitated for hard work, but of course it takes some little capital to get a license and to start a stand, and there is competition, and then it takes fair health for even that work, which requires being out of doors more or less in all kinds of weather.

This story is much like the preceding and both are given as examples of comfortable self-support.

No. 94—Mr. T.

Mr. T. I met at his trade of wandering street umbrella-mender. He said he earned about $7.00 a week and that he was separated from his wife and lived at a men's hotel. He was born in New York, is sixty-five years old, and said he was perfectly well. He looked as if he drank rather heavily, but perhaps his out-of-door life accounted partly for his appearance. He had worked on the docks and railroad, where he got $40.00 to $50.00 a month. He enjoys his present trade, as did another man, who earned about $4.00 a week, selling feather dusters all over New York. He said, however, he had no savings, which he ought to have, with $7.00 a week and no one else to support. He really is the sort of man one could see go to Blackwells Island without great regret, and yet he has a rather independent spirit, and I'd be sorry to send anyone to Blackwells Island.

Of these people described, it is easy to see that no one had a future really well assured, except perhaps No. 11, which is rather curious, because the single women of the investigation were mostly worse off than married people with children to depend on and than single men.

The special deduction to be drawn from this group is the uncertain future of most elderly people who are still working. They would not be working with their physical disabilities, many of them, if they had someone else to depend upon, and, therefore, when their present capacity for work gives out, as it soon will, they have no one on whom to rely for support.

III

AGED PEOPLE PARTLY SELF-SUPPORTING AND PARTLY SUPPORTED BY THEIR FAMILIES

THIS group contains nine persons. They are grouped as follows:

Six widows:

Three janitresses.
One takes lodgers.
One sews on skirts.
One does washing at home.

One single woman:

Dressmaker.

One married couple:

Longshoreman (husband).

One widower:

Mason and plasterer.

One of this group (a widow) is described in the chapter on "Difficulties of Saving for Old Age" (No. 68).

The following descriptions are given as the best illustrations of their group: two widows, the one single woman, the widower, and the couple.

No. 78—Mrs. M.

Mrs. M. is an Italian, seventy-five years old. She has been in New York fifteen years, but speaks very little English, as her daughter answered my questions altogether. She has rheumatism, but does sewing on cloth skirts. Her daughter said her mother had never worked except at home. She now lives with a son and his wife and one child, and the married daughter lives in the same house on another floor. The name was given me without any details, and I couldn't find out many details. I saw them working on the ready-made skirts, and apparently the family was able to care for the mother, only she was expected to work as long as possible. This illustration is given to show one of the ways that old women can help along a little when they have families able to take the larger part of their support.

No. 89—Mrs. P.

Mrs. P., a colored woman, sixty years old, having done laundry work in a laundry for years, now does occasional washings at home. She lives with two grandchildren, one seventeen years old, and they help her, as she doesn't make enough to support herself. As she says, "I've been sickly for ten years." Still, she probably makes enough to provide food for herself.

No. 18—Miss H.

Miss H., "over sixty," Irish, was a dressmaker, but now can't get much work, though she is well enough to sew. She lives alone, making what she can, and her sister contributes to her support. She spoke as if her sister could fairly easily help her, and she evidently likes living alone and gets on on a very small amount.

No. 40—Mr. S.

Mr. S. is an intelligent German, who has been in America thirty years.

At the time of his wife's death he had help from the C. O. S., and the two younger children were put in an orphanage. Now he and his sixteen-year-old daughter manage to live in an independent but poverty-stricken way. He had a trade-school training and worked as a builder. He once had his life insured, but failed to keep up payments and the policy lapsed. He has been incapacitated by severe asthma for years, but is occasionally able to do odd jobs as mason and plasterer. It is pathetic to see his various signs advertising his trade, because of course he can't be very competent now because of his failing strength and poor breathing, and, besides, the present-day demand is for younger men, who will work quickly, even if not so carefully or accurately.

So Mr. S. doesn't get much employment. His daughter began work at fourteen and now at sixteen has occasional factory work. She recently received $4.00 a week at a box factory, but as soon as a slack season arrived she was laid off. She isn't strong; has rheumatism and a weak heart. She has been advised to "live out," but she can't bear to leave her father, and he really does need her, as some of his attacks are very bad. Of course for a delicate girl to be so insufficiently fed and clothed is an economic waste, as she will inevitably become a care to society in an incurable hospital or some institution unless she dies. Her father chafes at his inability to support himself and her. He realizes she ought not to work, and yet they both need the money she earns at times. He has worked when he could, and evidently been steady and temperate. He is now a really tragic figure.

No. 71—Mr. G.

Mr. G., Irish, sixty years old, was at one time a second foreman, working on the White Star Company docks at $20.00 a week. Then he worked as a longshoreman, and now he gets only occasional jobs. He is well enough, but can't get much work. He partly supports himself, and he and his wife live with two sons, aged twenty-one and twenty-three, unmarried, and a widowed daughter with one child. His wife said, "It would set him crazy if he had to be dependent on his sons," but of course a little later it must come to that.

These illustrations (except Nos. 78 and 18) seem to indicate that the efforts of old people are required, even when they can only contribute a little to the family income. No. 40 may sound extreme, but is, in my opinion, a rather typical case.

I found that with only two or three exceptions old people do not give up working before they have to. On the whole, all worked who could possibly work.

IV

AGED PEOPLE SUPPORTED ENTIRELY BY THEIR FAMILIES

THIS group contains twenty-eight persons. They are grouped according to their last occupation.

Fifteen widows:

Four did washing.
Two did sewing.
One domestic nurse.
One did book-folding.
One was in an underwear factory.
One lived out.
Two never worked.
Three unclassified.

Two single women:

One curled feathers in a shop.
One was chambermaid in a hotel.

Seven couples:

One truck driver.
Three longshoremen.
One dock-worker.
One in tobacco factory.
One in sugar house, stableman and watchman.

Four widowers:

Two longshoremen.
One in factory.
One baker.

Several persons in this group are described elsewhere as follows: Two widows (Nos. 85 and 87), two couples (Nos. 31 and 95) and one widower (No. 60) in the chapter, "Effects of Dependency"; one widow (No. 10) in the chapter, "Difficulties of Saving"; one widow (No. 58), one longshoreman (No. 76), one couple (No. 97) and one widower (No. 92) in the chapter, "Causes of Dependency."

The following descriptions are given as the best illustrations of their group: three widows, one single woman, two couples and one widower.

No. 74—Mrs. K.

Mrs. K. is Irish, sixty-eight years old. She was a domestic servant till she married, and after her husband's death, twenty years ago, she worked in an underwear factory, but she hasn't been able to work for thirteen years on account of sickness and then feebleness.

She lives with a widowed daughter and her two children. There are no other relatives. The daughter makes $6.00 to $7.00 a week in a handkerchief factory. Seven dollars a week is not enough for two adults and two children; indeed it is most insufficient.

The two following cases seem especially good illustrations of families entirely willing to support the aged member, making no appeal for outside aid (unless having the service of a district visiting nurse is considered appealing to charity, and poor people don't consider it exactly that), while all the time an outsider can see the effects of under-nourishment and strain.

No. 54—Mrs. A.

Mrs. A. is from Sweden, a Protestant. She was a domestic laundress till she married, and her husband was a boiler-maker, who left no savings when he died. She is crippled and unable to work. She lives with a married daughter and her husband and two children. The son-in-law makes $12.00 a week. There are no other relatives. The mother and two young children look sickly. Twelve dollars a week is not enough to support a family of three adults and two children. They cannot possibly have enough to eat.

No. 66—Mrs. D.

Mrs. D., Irish, seventy-seven years old, lives with a daughter and son-in-law and six children. She has been a widow for eighteen years, and hasn't been able to work for fifteen years, which is natural, considering her age. The son-in-law is a truck-driver, making $12.00 a week. The youngest child is a baby, but think of three adults and five children living on $12.00 a week! They all looked sick and discouraged and dirty. The mother and daughter seemed to think the mother's dependence natural, but the son-in-law must feel it hard to support his mother-in-law when he isn't making enough to care for his children properly.

No. 41—Miss S.

Miss S. manages somehow to impress one with her dignity, even though she and her sister live in one back room in a furnished-room house on a disreputable and hopelessly dirty street. They are favored guests, in that the janitress gives them meals in the basement, and when Miss S. is unusually sick she has her meals on a tray upstairs, as she is seventy-eight. The younger sister is about sixty, but seems young in comparison and is still curling feathers in a shop. For a while during the spring she was laid off from work, and in trying a new temporary position she found that younger girls could work much faster, and was very thankful to regain her old job at $12.00 a week, out of which she pays $8.00 for board, i.e., for both her sister and herself. There is a brother of seventy-two, whose wife died recently, who has diabetes and gets a police pension of $14.00 per week (as a patrolman in service he made $1,200 a year). He had not helped the sisters, but perhaps he will now that his wife is dead after a long sickness. But he may die soon himself. The younger sister wishes that her sister would go into a Home, but won't suggest it to her, and is struggling hard to take care of her and support her. The older sister doesn't realize these struggles, and is full of pride over her sister's abilities. As she told me one day, " My sister is treasurer of the

—— club at the church, and when she wished to resign, the president simply would not allow it." The S.'s were born in New York, and have a feeling of responsibility for poorer neighbors. Once from the window I saw a man dressed in rags, sorting over the contents of the ash barrel in the backyard, and Miss S. exclaimed, "Oh, that is old Bismarck. He comes around every few days, and we give him pennies. He lives on the Bowery, and is supported by odd jobs and gifts. I haven't seen him for some time; no doubt we pamper him sometimes, and when he gets too many pennies he gets drunk." This was said with a grand air of kindly patronage. Poor women, they are both so really admirable and self-respecting—what is to be their fate!

No. 61—Mr. C.

Mr. C. is sixty-five years old, Irish, and an invalid with bad asthma. He was a longshoreman earning anywhere from $5.00 to $25.00 a week, towards the end only an average of $6.00 a week. But he hasn't been able to work for ten years on account of illness, and his wife can't work either.

They live with an unmarried son of twenty-four years, who makes only $8.00 a week. A married daughter, living in the same house with them, has six children and says she can't help her parents financially, but must, I think, help some. The man was too sick to talk, but the wife and daughter said they felt the situation "was hard" on the son and I quite agreed with them. I found the case through a nurse, and the family seemed independent and self-respecting. Savings were eaten up by the man's long illness, and now the two old people depend entirely on the son.

No. 82—Mr. M.

Mr. M. is Irish, sixty-seven years old. He was a longshoreman, and had no savings when he had a paralytic stroke eighteen years ago. He and his wife of sixty-one live with their son of twenty-two, unmarried, who works on the docks. I talked with the wife, who said her sister and cousins were the only other relatives and couldn't help, so their support falls entirely on the young son. She didn't say how much he made.

No. 96—Mr. T.

Mr. T. was born in Ireland and came to the United States when nineteen; now he is sixty. As a longshoreman he earned $12.00 to $20.00 a week—less as he grew older. His rheumatism made him give up work three years ago. He lost his wife eight months ago and lives with an unmarried daughter who works in a store. He has sisters in Brooklyn, but they can't help. He had no savings when he stopped work, but has some insurance. So the daughter must have had to support both parents for three years, and now has her father to care for entirely.

The special deduction from this group seems to be that the children show willingness to support their parents, but that they have many difficulties in so doing.

Many families are struggling so hard for a bare existence that even the smallest additional strain is a burden. Of course the old people do not eat a great deal, but their food costs something, and they take space which otherwise might bring in some income from boarders or lodgers.

This subject is taken up more fully in the chapter on "Effects of Dependency." The information was given me that Italian men usually retire very early and are supported by their children, but I did not happen to encounter this condition among the Italians I visited, perhaps because the ones I visited were poorer than those referred to; and certainly I did not find this the case with other nationalities.

On the whole, it seemed to me that the old people worked as long as possible and that their families struggled hard to support them when they could work no longer. In fact, it seemed as if the families' struggles were often too great, and that the whole economic standard of the families was thereby lowered.

V

AGED PEOPLE WHO ARE PARTLY SELF-SUPPORTING AND PARTLY DEPENDENT ON CHARITY

THIS group contains eight persons. They are grouped as follows, giving their occupation:

Six widows:

Two janitresses (at present).
One a former domestic nurse.
One does a little janitress work.
One does a little washing.
One helps one-third year in fresh air home.

One single woman:

Furnished rooms.

One single man:

Ladies' dressmaker.

One widow (No. 69) is described in the chapter, "Dislike of Institutions." The single man (No. 32) is described in the chapter, "Causes of Dependency."

The following descriptions are given here: Three widows and the single woman, as best illustrations of this group.

No. 23—Mrs. S.

Mrs. S. is seventy-four, a native of Germany. She said she stopped school at twelve years old to help her father, a tailor, working with him till she came to America, at the age of twenty-two. She then worked as a domestic servant till she married. Her husband was a glazier at $12.00 a week. He left no insurance.

She has "burial insurance." She works as a janitress for free rooms, and the A. I. C. P. gives her $5.00 a week for herself and two grandchildren. She had eight children. One daughter and three sons are left, but can't help her. She is soon to be moved by the Society to the Bronx and two other grandchildren are to live with her, and a general new arrangement is to be made. She has a most independent spirit and is hard-working and self-respecting.

No. 44—Mrs. T.

Mrs. T. is sixty-four, a native New Yorker in pretty good physical condition for her age. She does janitress work in a small house, which reduces the rent from $16.00 to $10.00 a month. Then she gets sewing from a church, from which she makes $1.00 a week, and receives an outright gift of 50 cents a week, so she is not dependent on her family, practically bringing in the equivalent of board and lodging. She lives with a widowed daughter who has a son of fourteen years. The daughter earns $10.00 a week and two meals daily, working in the restaurant at the Grand Central Station. This wage is good, but the hours are bad, from 2:30 in the afternoon to 12:30 at night, and the continual electric light and underground rooms are bad for her eyes and health generally. So it is well that the grandmother can help herself at present, and perhaps when the boy goes to work the mother can change to less harmful work, though the grandmother may not be able to do janitress work much longer. The sewing of course is charity, but she does not feel it that exactly.

No. 33—Mrs. N.

Mrs. N. is seventy, a native New Yorker. She never worked till fifteen years ago. Her husband died seventeen years ago, and she lived with her father, who had a U. S. Army pension, for two years. Then she did washing and still does a little, but makes only about 50 cents a week recently, as she is growing feeble. Her church gives her sewing, which brings her about $3.50

a week. She lives on this $4.00 a week, alone, paying $7.50 a month for rent and 50 cents a week for coal.

This case almost belongs with the group of people wholly dependent on charity, but I put it here as she earns a trifle. It and Case No. 26 in the next chapter, and others, show the part taken by church aid.

No. 15—Miss F.

Miss F. is a native New Yorker, seventy-five years old. She used to do sewing and tried renting furnished rooms, but wasn't successful and had no savings when she stopped regular work. She has now three rooms, rent $16.00 a month, and sublets one for $10.00. She gets $8.00 a month for church sewing, plus an outright gift of $2.00 a month, to which she adds with occasional odd jobs of sewing and washing. She feels she really earns the church money and calls herself "self-supporting." She won't go in a Home yet, but realizes she may have to do so some day. She thinks "women with husbands ought not to be given work," and it is true that an aged spinster has an especially hard time economically.

The special deduction from this group seems to be that old people, even when helped by charity, try to do what they can towards their own support, that there isn't that easy dependence on charity so many people fear. In the chapter, "Effects of Dependency," a sample case of a pauper family is given, a family (No. 28) ruined by charity, but this is given to be fair, to show all sides—not because I believe it represents an at all large class of people. Such a class I believe to be much smaller than is usually supposed. It was at any rate the only example among my one hundred cases investigated.

VI

AGED PEOPLE SUPPORTED PARTLY BY THEIR FAMILIES AND PARTLY BY CHARITY

THIS group contains thirteen people. They are grouped as follows, with their last occupations given:

Ten widows:

Three did washing.
One domestic servant.
One factory worker.
Two never worked.
Three unclassified.

One single woman:

Unclassified.

Two couples:

One painter.
One in appraiser's store—keeper at Blackwells Island.

One widow (No. 75) and one couple (No. 26) are described in the chapter, "Dislike of Institutions"; two widows (Nos. 3 and 28) are described in the chapter, "Effects of Dependency."

The following descriptions are given as the best illustrations of their group: four widows and the single woman.

No. 55—Mrs. A.

Mrs. A., Irish, aged sixty-five, has been a widow for nineteen years. She used to work in a crinoline skirt factory, getting $12.00 a week, but before she stopped she got only $4.00 a week at the Butterick factory. She had a fall and is feeble. She had no savings when she stopped work. She lives with her sister. The sister, also a widow, although only two years younger, is stronger and brighter, and still earns money at odd jobs. She was a milliner and also worked in a fruit store and a paper factory. A charitable society helps with groceries, and the two old women think that the "people at the office are just grand." When the younger one can't work, it looks as if an institution is all that is possible for them. Charitable societies rarely pension old people entirely, and as Catholics they can't get much help from their church.

No. 14—Mrs. F.

Mrs. F. is an Italian, aged sixty-two. She has been a widow since the age of twenty-five. She came to America eight years ago to join a prosperous son, but he has been stricken with blindness. The blind son is a widower with five children. One child was adopted, two are in Homes, and the other two live with their father and grandmother. One is sixteen and gets $5.00 a week, the other is fourteen and is trying for working papers. Another granddaughter, whose parents are in Italy, boards with the family. She is twenty-five years old, and works in a corset factory. A charitable association helps out. Again it seems as if the burden fell heavily on the young.

No. 47—Mrs. W.

Mrs. W. is Irish, sixty-seven years old. She isn't strong physically or mentally and cannot work any. Her husband was an iron-moulder, who died seven years ago. She said she never knew how much he earned! She lives with a son of fourteen, at work, and a feeble-minded daughter. Another feeble-minded child is at Central Islip. She is helped by a charitable association, but the responsibility for the young son seems heavy.

No. 19—Mrs. H.

Mrs. H. I found living with a daughter whose husband had died very recently, and whose son of fifteen was making $3.50 a week. Unfortunately I forgot to find out if the daughter who was looking for work had found any, but she could probably find something in time, and the church to which they belonged was helping them. The point of this illustration is that Mrs. H. has been a widow for twelve years and her husband was ill for fifteen years before he died, with diabetes, and Mrs. H. has the same malady. Think of the burden of such long illnesses, for poor people!

No. 26—Miss M.

Miss M., sixty years old, born in New York, lives with her sister, who makes $7.50 a week at a collar and cuff laundry. She receives help from her church, about $4.00 a week from sewing and outright gifts. She has epilepsy and cannot do any real work. If it were not for the church's assistance it would be a very difficult case, as the sister's $7.50 is scarcely enough to support two people, one an invalid. She is rather above most of the people in this investigation, and yet not equal to some, and not eligible for one of the better-class Homes, even if her infirmity did not bar her out.

The special deductions from this group seem to be that families do not take more outside assistance for their aged members than is necessary, and that churches and charitable societies have many demands for help for the aged which they consider entirely reasonable and right.

The few men in these last two groups, and the next group, will be commented upon in the conclusions after the next group.

VII

AGED PEOPLE WHOLLY DEPENDENT ON CHARITY

THIS chapter includes two groups. The first group contains nine persons with their past occupations as follows:

Five widows:

Three did sewing.
One milliner.
One unclassified.

Three single women:

One sewing.
One factory work.
One fur worker.

One couple:

Shoemaker.

Of these, two widows (Nos. 4 and 29) are described in the chapter, " Dislike of Institutions "; one widow (No. 7) is described in the chapter, " Effects of Dependency," and one single woman (No. 12) in the chapter, " Difficulties of Saving."

The following descriptions are given as the best illustrations of their group: two widows, one single woman and the couple.

No. 34—Mrs. O'H.

Mrs. O'H. was born in Ireland. She is seventy, and seems weak physically and mentally. Her husband died thirty-four years ago. She lives with an unmarried daughter of thirty. An unmarried son, a machinist, died three years ago. The daughter had to give up factory work on account of tuberculosis, and now one of the charitable societies is helping them. The daughter evidently wasn't a bad case of tuberculosis, as she is supposed to be nearly well; but it all seemed rather hopeless to me, for if the daughter goes back to work in a factory she is apt to have the trouble again worse than ever. She said to me, " Factory work is hard; indeed, all life seems just hurry up, hurry up."

No. 77—Mrs. L.

Mrs. L. was born in America, and is a widow, aged sixty-two. Before marriage she was a milliner, and also after her husband's death. His sickness used up his money. She ranged in earnings $10.00, $18.00, $12.00, $10.00 a week. She is incapacitated now because of sciatica and rheumatism. She has no children and no relatives nearer than second cousins, and lives alone in a " furnished room." She is supported by her church, which pays her rent, and by friends who contribute food. She evidently doesn't get enough food. She said, " I stinger myself as much as possible." A working-woman I knew well vouched for her as a thoroughly hard-working, admirable woman.

No. 25—Miss M.

Miss M. lives in proud isolation, scorning her neighbors, for, as she said to me one day, " How would you like to live with people a class below yours? " She has one room and an alcove, and refuses to be friends even with the woman next door, who is supported by the same church! She said of this neighbor, " She insulted me one day, and I sent her out of my room and told her never to come back," adding with tears in her eyes, " But I am sociable and try to go out to see people, though I'm too nervous to see people who irritate me." Poor soul, she has nervous dyspepsia and is feeble and a cataract has grown over one eye. Because she has " seen better days," the church to which she belongs is most generous to her, spending upon her about $25.00

a month for rent, food, heat, etc. In contrast to others in the house she is very comfortable, but she does not think she is comfortable; her scorn of her surroundings is intense. Her father was in business, but failed when she was eleven years old. Without any real training she worked in stores and factories, and at one time earned $18.00 a week, in seasonal work, but eight years ago she had to stop work on account of her poor eyesight. She can't see to read much now, says she repeats poetry she learned when a child in Canada, and she goes to lectures at the public schools, etc. She once said, "I used to go to lectures at school—but the only lectures they have now are *economical,* and I have enough of that at home, and I don't like it!" She is a keen observer of character, and one day in commenting upon one of her church visitors, she said, "Miss —— never lost herself"—a rather neat comment on self-control, I thought! With all her loneliness and unhappiness she won't go into a Home, and it is fortunate she is a member of a church able to support her.

No. 46—Mr. V.

Perhaps old Mr. and Mrs. V. do take charity a little easily now, having lost the capacity to provide for themselves years ago. If you were seventy-seven and partly paralyzed, wouldn't you feel as if someone ought to take care of you, and if you had no children, or anyone to depend upon, wouldn't you fall back on charity and finally get used to it? I can't put Mr. V. quite in the "pauper class." He was born in Germany, where he learned the trade of shoemaker, and he worked in Switzerland and France before coming to America. When he had to give up working he had $500 saved, but of course that would not last so very long. A Home that sometimes gives outside aid gives him and his wife $15.00 a month. They pay $5.00 a month for two rooms in a rear tenement ground-floor, damp and drafty. That leaves $10.00 a month for some food and fuel, light, clothes, etc. Another charity gives them weekly groceries and occasional gifts, but is trying to persuade them to go into a Home. However, they prefer to be together and independent, no matter how uncomfortable. What a travesty on Browning's words,

> " Grow old along with me,
> The best is yet to be,
> The last of life, for which the first was made! "

this picture is, of cold, half-starved people, with lives empty, forlorn and neglected!

The special deduction from this group seems to be that people who are given entire support by charitable societies and churches really do need it. None of the people in this group are really to blame for their dependence.

I was impressed by the fact that I found a number of single women and widows, but few men, living alone, and that I found more women than men that were entirely dependent. I wondered if men, who naturally have not as much of the " home-making instinct " as women and therefore would not try to live alone, cooking for themselves, would drift out of Greenwich Village, down to the cheap Bowery hotels and lodging-houses. But a clerk in a cheap men's hotel in lower Greenwich Village said that his place was as cheap as those in the Bowery, and that I must remember that men incapacitated for work and without wives, children or sisters, were apt to give up and go to the Island, and that men of the very poorest classes often drank heavily and died early. Therefore there are not as many elderly men helped by outdoor charity as women.

Later at a men's hotel, of a slightly better grade, on Sixth Avenue I did learn that there were a good many men there over sixty, able to work a little, so it is true that instead of trying to live alone, if they have a little money men go to a hotel.

It can easily be understood that more elderly poor women than men would be members of churches and helped by them. One church in Greenwich Village has a list of about twenty elderly women who are partly or wholly dependent on the church's bounty, and they are an especially deserving group.

And it is easy to see that single persons are more apt to be dependent than people with children, and especially single women, because they are more unselfish, as a whole, in helping their relatives from time to time and therefore less apt to accumulate savings.

And there are many widows whose children are dead, and their position is much like that of single women.

And then, too, there are many married women who have never worked, or at least not during their husband's lifetime, who find it difficult to support themselves after their husband's death. Those who have worked before marriage generally cannot go back to the same kind of work, having lost in efficiency during the intervening years, except in unskilled work like scrubbing offices, etc.

Apparently the poorer workingmen can't or won't keep up life insurance,—probably they can't, most of them,—and often men better off won't, so widows of men with good wages, and sometimes of men with good salaries, are utterly destitute.

The subject of the cost of maintenance of people outside of institutions is discussed in the chapter, "Dislike of Institutions."

The second group in this chapter perhaps really does not belong here. It is a group of people who receive U. S. Army pensions, who otherwise would necessarily be entirely supported by charity. Of the one hundred investigated three others than those in this group received U. S. Army pensions, but as they were also helped by their families they are included in the group, "Aged People Supported Partly by Their Families and Partly by Charity."

This group numbers six persons as follows, with last occupations:

Five widows:

One never worked.
One tailoress.
One dressmaker.
One did washing and janitress work.
One unclassified.

One widower:

Worked in Navy Yard, and on bridges.

One widow (No. 90) is described in the chapter, "Causes of Dependency," and the widower (No. 99) in the chapter, "Difficulties of Saving."

As an illustration of this group, the following description is given as typical:

No. 88—Mrs. P.

Mrs. P. I met on the street and, after some conversation, accompanied to her home. She is Irish, seventy-seven years old. She was a tailoress before she married. Her husband was a brass finisher. He was in the Civil War for three years, during which time bad kidney trouble developed, so that afterward he could do very little work. After his death Mrs. P. did washing and ironing, but now she has severe rheumatism and can't work. She had four children; one was lost in the army, one is in an asylum, two daughters live in Brooklyn, but evidently can't or won't help her. A grandson lives with her and pays $4.00 a week board, but practically the pension supports her. (The usual U. S. war pension for a widow is $12.00 a month.)

The special deduction from this group seems to be that as these few people actually need their war pensions, perhaps others receiving war pensions do also. But in no way do I wish to seem to approve the reckless extension of our war pensions, as I know that many, many people receive them who do not need them.

The question naturally arises why the victims of war and their wives should receive pensions any more than industrial victims. In this connection I wish to quote from Jacob H. Hollander's recent book, "The Abolition of Poverty." He says (p. 105): "A very considerable part of those in receipt of pensions lie without the ranks of the aged poor, and, on the other hand, certain large categories from whom this class is largely recruited, are entirely excluded from the benefits of the pension system. The real significance lies in the fact that the

United States has for nearly two generations been making generous expenditures—in 1912 the cost of the pension system was $153,000,000, about three times as great as that of the British old-age pension system—which, even though originally inspired by other considerations, have as their actual consequence the relief of a material part of existing old-age dependence. Both in fiscal provision and in public preparedness, the way has been paved for a transition to a more comprehensive, a more equitable, and probably a more economical, system of old-age provision."

VIII

CAUSES OF DEPENDENCY OF THE AGED

THE causes of old-age dependency are found upon inquiry to be many and varied, and upon the whole much more pardonable than would seem on the surface. Dependency can be traced principally to the following causes: (1) to lack of proper industrial training in youth; (2) to low wages during the entire working period; (3) to the specialization of industry; (4) to casual employment or non-employment stretching over a fairly long period of time; (5) to diseases caused by under-nourishment, overcrowding and overstrain; (6) to dangerous occupations and industrial accidents; (7) to the natural feebleness and inefficiency which old age naturally brings, in reality and in general estimation, for even if old people are not weak and inefficient they are so considered and younger men especially are preferred by employers, and the younger generation crowds out the older; (8) to intemperance, although, as Frank H. Streightoff says in "The Standards of Living Among the Industrial People of America" (p. 147), "Alcohol is both the cause and the effect of bad conditions of living"; and (9) to the death of the breadwinner of the family, leaving families unable to support themselves.

Before giving illustrations from the lives of people with whom I came in contact during the investigation, I wish to quote from two writers on this subject. The first quotation refers to dependent widows with young children, but really it is also applicable to older people, and sums up the general causes of poverty, which of course eventually make older people dependent. Edward T. Devine, in his "Report of an Investigation on Matters Relating to the Care, Treatment, and Relief of Dependent Widows with Dependent Children," says (pp. 35, 36):

"The second explanation to be considered for the lack of improvement in some families—and here we are upon surer ground—is that the overwhelming mass of human misery, of which the suffering and dependence in these few thousand families of widows is but a part, is the result of causes and conditions with which both voluntary charity and public relief as such are powerless to deal. Tuberculosis, typhoid, fatal industrial injuries, insufficient pay, economic inefficiency, the physical strain of overwork, the exploitation of the vices and weaknesses of men and women for commercial profit, are all subjects with which social workers in the charitable societies are deeply concerned, but for which remedies lie in other and more powerful hands. Concerning the great creative forces of the misery which they are called upon to investigate and relieve in individual instances they can only lift up their voices in eloquent testimony. They may testify also, as has been intimated, to human weaknesses, to lack of energy and resistance, to the fact that some human beings are apparently from their birth doomed to failure in any severe life-struggle. But they may well be appalled when they see such weaker persons, and others not by any means unfit for any reasonable struggle, subjected to uncontrolled infection, to overcrowding, to overwork, and injurious strain, to fiendish temptations such as the strongest could not resist under similar circumstances, to a necessity of paying the highest price for inferior, diluted and polluted commodities and services, and to further necessity of providing from their own insufficient resources and by their own inadequate efforts, for such contingencies as sickness and death in the family, for childbirth, for infirmity and old age, for unemployment, whether due to personal fault and inefficiency or to industrial causes affecting an entire group or an entire community of workers. The large lesson to be learned from any such study of the widows' problems as has been made for this committee is that of the responsibility of the community for much of the larger part of the sickness, death and dependence which constitute that problem, and the utter inadequacy of either public or voluntary relief as a solution of that problem.

Until the community responsibilities for the social and industrial causes of poverty are more fully met it will be unreasonable to expect either public-relief officials or voluntary agencies to secure a reasonable standard of living or normal family life for any large proportion of those whom they seek to aid. The charitable agencies do, however, come to have a large amount of valuable evidence of the need for preventive social measures, and their leaders have been conspicuous in initiating and advocating such action."

The second quotation, although it refers especially to old men, can be applied also to old women.

In the book " One Thousand Homeless Men," by Alice W. Solenberger, in the chapter on Homeless Old Men (p. 112), she says: " Eighty-five of the 132, as has been said, were of good character and habits, and had always, previous to the advent of old age, been self-respecting and fully self-supporting members of society. With these men the causes which were apparently most responsible for their final dependence were (1) the receipt of irregular and insufficient wages over a period of years, which made saving for age difficult if not impossible; (2) the rearing of families which had exhausted resources and in the end left no member able to care for the parents; (3) impracticability or lack of 'business sense,' on the part of upright and industrious men; (4) loss of savings through bank failures; (5) business reverses for which the men themselves could not be blamed; (6) ill-health or crippling accidents which destroyed earning capacity before sufficient savings for age had been accumulated, and a few other miscellaneous causes, none of which indicated failure upon the part of the men themselves to do their best during their working years to prepare for oncoming age."

Here are a few illustrations from the hundred studied in this investigation, which best show some of the causes of dependency mentioned.

No. 58—Mrs. C.

Mrs. C. is a native American, aged seventy-eight. She has never done any regular work. Her husband worked in the Knickerbocker Ice Co., but was killed thirty-seven years ago in an accident. The firm paid her $300 and took her oldest child of seventeen (she had five younger children) into their employ, and he became a bookkeeper. She has three children living; three daughters, two of whom are married, and she lives with the unmarried one, who makes only $7.00 a week. Perhaps the married daughters contribute something to the mother's support, but she says, "I don't know what I would do if it weren't for this daughter," referring to the unmarried one. Of course nowadays in New York a firm would have to provide an annuity for such a widow, but this is not yet the case in most American states.

No. 90—Mrs. R.

Mrs. R., born in the United States, is seventy years old, a widow who has never worked any. Her husband was a church sexton and Civil War veteran who died six months ago after an illness lasting five years. They had no children and had saved money, but that was lost in an unfortunate investment. She is lame, having fallen and broken her hip. Her two sisters, both widows, can't help her, and she gets along on the $12.00 a month war pension with a little help from her church. As she says, it is difficult to pay rent and for coal and food out of $12.00 a month. She has two tiny rooms in an attic for $6.00 a month and lives alone. She says, "What would I do without the pension?" She did not say what the investment was or how it was lost.

No. 36—Mrs. Q.

Mrs. Q. is English. She came to America when thirty-eight, and is now over sixty; still she hasn't grown at all American, and seems to have walked straight out from the pages of a Dickens novel. She is in good physical and mental condition; indeed, she is really clever. At one time she did drink quite a little, but has straightened up again. She is supported largely by church sewing and gifts from friends, but in the summer has a position at a Fresh-Air Home. She says she is on the "night-watch" for three months. She lives alone, but has numerous friends at settlements as well as at her church. After a curious career she is now satisfied and happy. She feels she has always worked hard, and now that she can't do any regular work she feels it right for the church to help her. Her father was a pawn-broker, and she was always comfortable at home. She married a Scotland Yard detective, and they came to America. Her husband apparently never worked much in America. She had two successful little dry-goods stores, said she sometimes made $200 a month, but lost $1,200 in an investment. Her husband made her very unhappy; he was wild and unfaithful to her, and so extravagant he used up all her savings. After his death, which was a great relief to her, she tried running a furnished-room house, but was not very successful in that venture, and finally gave up trying to support herself. People can't help feeling sorry for her, and are glad now that she should be so happy, after her many vicissitudes. She goes to many meetings and sociable affairs at her church and two settlements, and is always an important figure. Her appreciation of speeches is unusually keen, and she is always impressive and entertaining and would really be missed in her community if she had to go away to an institution.

No. 78—Mrs. T.

Mrs. T. is Irish, sixty, and a widow. She used to work in a store, and then as a chambermaid in a hotel at $10.00 a month with board. She hasn't been able to work for ten years, as she has had kidney trouble and varicose veins and suffers a great deal. She lives with a cousin who supports her, though she herself is nearly sixty and makes only $7.00 a week. Mrs. T. has no other relatives, and appreciates her cousin's kindness very much. The cousin also pays for Mrs. T.'s insurance, the principal of which is soon due. Perhaps that will help them both, as probably the cousin can't work much longer. Mrs. T. feels her dependence very much, but naturally her savings were used up during her ten years' illness.

No. 97—Mr. T.

Mr. and Mrs. T. live with an unmarried daughter of nineteen who works in a biscuit factory, and they have a boarder. Mr. T. was born in New York sixty-two years ago. He worked in a tobacco factory, where he made $12.00 to $14.00 a week until five years ago, when his hands were injured. His wife said he "feels bad because he can't work," but really there are few things that a man of sixty-two with deformed hands can do. He might be a "ticket-chopper" on the elevated road, but these jobs are difficult to get, or he might have some sort of street stand, but these take money to start.

No. 92—Mr. S.

Mr. S., Irish, a widower, aged seventy-eight, is deaf and feeble and unable to work. He was a baker, but had to give up his trade on account of sickness fifteen years ago. He made $13.00 to $15.00 a week, but had no savings when he stopped. He lives with his sister (all his other relatives are dead), who keeps boarders and supports him as well as herself. She said that her brother worked as long as he could, but now takes his dependency on her as natural, and she feels it is "rather hard."

No. 32—Mr. McI.

Mr. McI. is both typical and unique—typical in that he represents a class of men thrown out of employment, partly by being pushed out by younger men and partly by having a trade that is growing obsolete, and unique because of his present mode of existence and support. He is a native New Yorker, single, aged sixty-seven. He is in good physical and mental condition. I made only one call on him and his sister, but was so entertained I wished to go again. I found her—she is seventy-three—cooking the dinner, and he was sewing on the machine, doing sewing given to his sister by the church. When I asked how he was able to do that kind of sewing he told me his story. As a young man he had tuberculosis, and when he recovered he could not do heavy work, so he became a woman's dressmaker (not tailor) and followed that trade for thirty-four years. He spoke with pride of dressmaking done for actresses, such minor ones that I failed to recognize their names, but tried not to show my ignorance. He showed me a waist he had made his sister, as a sample of his work, and it was certainly a marvelous creation. But he said, "Nowadays people buy ready-made clothing; it's cheaper." So he gets work only occasionally. He and his sister have two rooms for $11.00 a month, and she gets $3.00 worth of sewing a week and a gift of fifty cents a week, which probably pays the rent and for her food, and he probably makes enough for his food. And he does most of her sewing. He is said to be a kind good man, and his pride, though amusing, also has something fine about it—to love work, even if dressmaking work, is to share in the dignity of labor to some extent! He is still proud of his profession and of his figure, and his small wrist, and he is bright and cheerful, and he and his sister seem happy together. But if it were not for the church assistance what would they do?—for neither could really earn money at regular work.

Of course the locality of Greenwich Village and the limited number of people studied cannot furnish illustrations of all the causes of dependency, but these descriptions are given as examples of some of the causes, and other experiences and testimony bear out the facts stated at the beginning of the chapter.

At the Salvation Army headquarters in Greenwich Village I was told that the men who applied there for work confessed that they dyed their hair to appear younger, and that men were often thrown out of work, not because of incompetence, but simply because of their age.

One woman nearly sixty (No. 41 in Chapter IV.) told me that during a slack season she was laid off her usual job and tried to work elsewhere, and that she found it difficult to compete with young women; as she sadly said, "I find they can work faster; I fear I can't hold the job." Later, much to her relief, she was called back to her old place. She is well and strong, but simply hasn't the nerves or the skillful fingers for the speed which modern industry demands.

At St. Vincent's Hospital I was told that few elderly men applied at the dispensary, because "The majority of men in Greenwich Village are longshoremen and truck drivers, and the former are not only injured often, but often die early."

A tenement inspector told me "Many of the women in Greenwich Village do laundry work and that leads to rheumatism and Bright's disease."

Some men do change from one kind of work to another, in an ascending and then a descending scale of wages, but some men who have all their lives done but one kind of work, when that line is obsolete or overcrowded, know nothing else to do, and can find only the poorest kind of badly paid work to go into—if they find any work. This is one of the results of specialization of industry.

As an example of this there is the following story: Two or three years ago the husband in a little family I was interested in, in Greenwich Village, lost his job in a tobacco factory where he had been practically ever since he left school. He was not discharged—but the firm failed. He was about twenty-eight years old, born of Italian parents in this country, undersized and not strong (how could he be? he had scarcely ever had plenty of really nourishing food). His wife, an American, had worked in the same factory at times, but had two children and another one was expected. The man tried in vain to get work, and people in his wife's church tried also to help him find work. Finally I enlisted the help of a workingman, who interviewed a boss in a factory where he had once worked, in behalf of Mr. G., but poor little G. wasn't able to do any heavy work and had no skill whatever except in his own line. The older workingman said, "I'm trying hard to get that young fellow a job; he is just the kind that should not be out of work long. He will get discouraged, and then he will go to pieces." Finally the church took him in some of its work, and paid him more than he was really worth. He had no initiative, and no resource and no general skill, as a natural result of his specialized work.

Now, if people are incompetent when young, what can we expect of them when they grow old? It is not people's fault often when they are incompetent, but a lack in their early training or in their one-sided occupations, and very frequently in their lack of physical energy. It is utterly unreasonable to expect energy and initiative and skill from a man with no training mentally or industrially, and with a weak constitution. So then, incompetency becomes often not so much the fault of individuals as the fault of our social system.

One of the usual remarks of the careless and uninformed is: "Oh, of course any man who is of any account can get a good job." But I've tried desperately hard to find work for competent men as well as incompetent men, and here also find amazing difficulties.

Again, it is easy to talk of men rising, but often if a man has any fairly good job, or even a poor one, he is afraid (if he is married) to run any risk of losing that job by trying for a better job, and thus his ambition is deadened.

A workingman (not in New York, but the situation is no doubt universal) said once to me, "Some of the men at the works thought I was crazy to risk giving up my job there till I had another one somewhere else; poverty makes cowards of them." But this man was able to take the risk and give up the work that was undermining his health because influence was being used to procure work for him elsewhere, and because assistance for his family was assured in the interim between the two jobs. But the man with no backing hasn't the time or opportunity even to apply for work elsewhere, and doesn't dare risk interims between jobs. And so men stay in one position, or one kind of work, all their lives, which gives them temporary support and in no way provides for their old age, but this is discussed further in the chapter, "Difficulties of Saving." Enough has been said here to indicate the general causes of dependency.

IX

DIFFICULTIES OF SAVING FOR OLD AGE

IN the preceding chapter the subject of low wages was touched upon, but I wish to dwell upon it more at length here, because it seems to me very few realize that the poor have practically no margin for unexpected demands, much less for savings, with their small budgets.

A very clever Irish woman of good birth whom I have known for years, whose husband, once rich through lucky speculations in another country, is now poor and forced into the ranks of unskilled workers, once said to me, apropos of her husband's wage at that time of $11.00 a week (with a family of four children), " I now understand Lord Roberts' remark about the 'irreducible minimum'! "

Another woman, who told me she could live well on $12.00 a week when they had that, was, on the very surface, an example refuting that statement. She and her husband and two children were living in three rooms (two of which were dark), and all were undersized and looked under-nourished, and were sick a great deal.

When people haven't enough for the daily necessities of life, how can they save?

Let me quote here from Louise Boland More, who lived two years at Greenwich House, and wrote as a result of her investigations a book, " Wage-Earners' Budgets." She says on p. 5: " The average wage-earner's family in this neighborhood is constantly on the verge of dependence, and would become dependent on friends or charity, at any time of long-continued industrial depression, illness, or unemployment. The 'margin of surplus' of the income over expenditures is very small, and it is only in exceptional cases that it is possible for a family of average size to make much provision for the future."

It is intensely instructive to follow the career of an unskilled workingman's family for a period of several years, encountering its various vicissitudes. A family which I have known for about eight years has lived all up and down the west side of New York and Harlem, and is now in Brooklyn. The man never makes more than $12.00 a week as a driver or at other casual occupations, and very often he is on part-time work or out of work. At one time, having sold all their furniture, the family were reduced—the five of them—to living in one "furnished room," for which they paid $4.00 a week. At this juncture a more fortunate friend, giving up a furnished lodging-house, offered them some furniture if they could get into a flat in which to put it.

There are various Protestant churches that lend funds to parishioners, but this family is Roman Catholic, and the Penny Provident Fund and other such societies require some sort of guarantee. As the family had appealed too often to the charitable societies, they would not help. I found the $17.00 with which to pay rent in advance and to move the furniture. Since then they have never reverted to such destitution, though several times since they have received groceries from a charitable society, and one other time I paid two-thirds rent for them, and a Catholic priest paid the remaining one-third and sent men to move them. The oldest son now has work and two other children will be able to get their working papers in a year or two, and the wife often takes the position of janitress. But, unfortunately, when the boy has work the man often hasn't, or, if both are working, back debts have to be paid and generally someone is sick, and thus an extra expense. They occasionally catch up in their finances, but they never really get ahead.

The man has two or three times in these last eight years lost his job because of drinking, but on the whole since taking a cure when I first knew him, he has kept pretty steady, even through periods of discouragement and times of such inadequate nourishment that I trembled for his good resolutions.

I have described this family at length because it seems to me to illustrate in a concrete way the unceasing struggle to "keep even." How could such a family have a "margin of surplus," much less save anything?

In a way this family epitomizes the sort of existence a large proportion of our humbler wage-earners lead—forever hovering on the brink of destitution, always making an effort to have enough to eat and a decent place in which to sleep, and yet seldom achieving even that, being forever underfed, usually badly housed, and often in overcrowded quarters.

This case, although it may have some distinctive features, must be typical of thousands and thousands of people.

Various statistics have been compiled giving the lowest budget on which workingmen's families can possibly exist.

John R. Shillady in an article in *The Survey* says: "The Committee on Standards of Living and Labor of the National Conference of Charities and Correction has been formulating standards below which society dare not go and be safe. These standards have been accepted by the conscience of the country, so far as the social workers of the country represent that conscience, as a minimum for industry. The Pittsburg Survey, Chapin's study for New York, the New York State Conference figures for 1907, and other investigations have convinced even the sceptical that less than $800 in New York, between $635 and $700 in Buffalo five years ago, and approximately the same amounts in other places are unsafe minimums for a family of five. The 1912 platform of the National Conference Committee asked, among other things, enough to provide for a normal standard of living; to provide for recreation and amusement, etc." And yet a large per cent of workingmen receive a wage of less than $600 a year.

So much for quotations as to wages and their testimony as to the difficulties of providing a living, still less a budget on which savings are possible. Does it not seem reasonable to decide that many families simply cannot save, and that when families do save it is at a tremendous cost to themselves, and to society indirectly, in bringing about low standards of living and also often low standards of morals? This effect of income on morals is well summed up by J. R. Shillady in the article in *The Survey* referred to before. He says: "Character, efficiency and a high standard of living are among the main things of life, but they are not achieved first in serial order but only after income has been secured. Though all persons with adequate incomes do not possess 'character' and 'efficiency,' or achieve a high standard of living from every point of view, yet, on the whole, increase of income, when assured and permanent from sources not demoralizing, results in higher standards, greater efficiency and better character. Incomes falling below an amount sufficient to provide for the normal demands of the human animal for food, shelter and recreation, result in decreased efficiency, lowered standards and weakened character."

From years of personal experience with the poor, it is astonishing to me that individuals do preserve, even when in most dire poverty, as much moral stamina as they do.

And even when people have larger incomes these may be cut down by heavy expenses for sickness, accidents and occasional non-employment.

In the hundred people investigated, only a few were found that had any savings, and these were not large enough to last long. And the few who had these savings had received higher wages than the others, or had had fewer demands upon them because of no families, or small families to support.

And added to low wages and accidents, illnesses and non-employment which eat up savings, there are instances of bad investments.

It is of very little benefit to theorize about people and to say that they should be different. Poor people might perhaps be much more efficient in finding good jobs and in keeping them when found, and in keeping well and in spending their wages more wisely, but in our efforts to help them we must face the situation as it is, and we must not expect impossibilities from them. Indeed, considering all their difficulties, I am often amazed that they manage as well as they do.

The following descriptions are given as illustrations of the subject:

No. 68—Mrs. D.

One of the Catholic churches gave me Mrs. D.'s name. I found her scrubbing some rear tenement steps, very breathless because she has asthma. She is sixty-two, born in Ireland, but has been in New York since she was twelve years old. Her husband was a blacksmith, and she had five children, but they are all dead. She did washing and cleaning before and after her husband's death, and now is a janitress. She said she was paid only $6.00 for her work, and pays $4.00 in addition for her rent, i.e. she gets by her work $6.00 off the $10.00 a month rent.

That seemed rather impossible at first, but I learned that janitress' compensations vary greatly—from rooms plus money, to rooms for which there must be some payment made. It depends on the size of the house and whether furnace care is included, and also seems to vary with different landlords' or agents' wills, and the bargain they can make. Two widows of my hundred people got rooms free for work, and two other widows besides Mrs. D. got reduced rent, and two couples working together got rooms plus money.

Mrs. D. must get fees from other people in the tenement where she is janitress, and her brother, who "works on a boat," helps her, as she must make the $4.00 extra for rent, and get money for food. She is unusually clean and brave and patient and hard-working, but naturally how can she save anything?

No. 93—Mrs. T.

Mrs. T.'s tale is tragic. Her pastor spoke of her with respect when he gave me her name, and after my one call I left her with admiration. It is difficult to decide where to place her as an illustration—for she illustrates the self-supporting group, and is an example of the difficulties of saving and a person one would hate to send to an institution when she can work no longer. She was born in New York City sixty years ago, and learned the dressmaking trade with her mother, leaving school at fourteen. She followed her trade till she married, and since her husband's death, after a severe illness, six years ago. She had seven sons, but they are all dead, and she has no other relatives and no savings. She used to make $8.00 to $9.00 a week years ago, but now her income is most uncertain. She says she occasionally makes $30.00 a month, but she has taken in as little as $2.50 a month. She lives alone, and her health is good, and she seems young for her age, which is remarkable, for according to her accounts the cases of illness of members of her family which she has nursed would have worn most women out utterly. I stopped her recital of illnesses, and said, "You are wonderful to have lived through all that," and she replied, "Oh, I haven't told you half of all I've gone through." Now, probably she cannot sew till the very end of her life, and, even if she could, it is difficult to believe her neighbors would continue to employ an old woman as a dressmaker in competition with cheap ready-made clothes! What is to become of her? How could such a woman ever save money?

No. 10—Mrs. D.

Mrs. D., Irish, sixty years old, lives with a son of eighteen, who works with the Western Electric Company and makes $15.00 a week. She feels after former greater comfort that it is very difficult to manage on that, but their present position isn't the point of this illustration, nor is the fact that she herself at one time earned $12.00 to $15.00 a week at book-folding. The point is, that her husband after such a good position as he had left her nothing. He made $25.00 a week and fees in a hotel (he had something to do with managing waiters and keeping books, etc., at entertainments; I couldn't quite understand just what he did, but he got good fees as well as a salary). And the reason he left her nothing was that he was sick four years before he died, and as she said, "All his earnings were eaten up."

No. 12—Miss D.

Miss D., Irish, aged sixty-two, was a hand worker on furs. Her highest pay was $10.00 a week. She had savings, but they were used up by illness in her family. She has trouble with her arms now and can't do anything but church sewing, and sewing from a society, and out of what she makes she helps a widowed sister, who lives with two worthless nephews, as the third sister is dead. All the money she has ever made has had to be used for others. How could she save?

No. 39—Mr. R.

Mr. R. is an Italian, sixty-six years old, who came to the United States when ten years old. As a child he went about with his father and a "grind organ." Then he went into a candy factory for sixteen years, and finally had an independent artificial flower business—in the best years making a profit of $6,000 according to his daughter's account. Then three years ago the business went into a receiver's hands, "because of someone else's fault." Now because of his chronic asthma and feebleness he can't work. He has enough savings to support himself and his wife for about one year, and they are to move to a little house of their own on Bath Beach. There are eight sons and two daughters, and they can support their parents when the savings give out, but this shows how difficult it is to have savings to last many years, even after a profitable business career.

No. 99—Mr. W.

Mr. W., Scotch, seventy-eight, widower, came to America when fifteen years old. He was a sailor at $16.00 a month, and was in the Navy during the War. Then he worked in the Navy Yard at $3.50 a day, and finally worked on bridges at $4.50 a day, and even for $1.50 an hour for some specially dangerous work. A year ago he hurt his head working on a bridge and hasn't worked since, but he draws a Navy pension of $22.50 a month, on which he lives comfortably. He said he tried a Home, but left it and lives in a room somewhere, taking his meals at a restaurant. He has no near relatives. It would seem as if he could have saved money, but he said no, that he had $1,800 in the bank at one time, but his wife's last sickness used that up! This was a street acquaintance, but the story sounds plausible.

To show how and why some people *can* save money, the following illustrations are given—Nos. 62 and 56—which are unusual cases.

No. 62—Mr. C.

Mr. C., met on the street, gave the following report: He was born in Italy, but has lived in America forty years, is now sixty-eight years old, and is single. He had a peanut and fruit stand, but gave it up two and one-half years ago because of sickness and lameness. He has savings and boards with friends. He seems to have been able to save because he had no family in America and could keep all he made for himself!

No. 56—Mr. A.

Mr. A. is a native American, aged seventy-two. He is in good physical condition, and is still working. His wife is dead and he has two unmarried sons, both living with him and working. He has some savings—why? Because he is a skilled laborer—a bricklayer—and his family has not been a great strain on him. He sometimes made $7.00 a day, or $50.00 a week, and now gets 70 cents an hour. Of course, bricklaying is a seasonal occupation, or at least not a steady one, but he has done well in it, and evidently he has not been ambitious, having been content to live on Jones Street for twenty-five years.

Then there is one more difficulty which the poor experience in trying to make wages cover their needs and leave a little over for emergencies if not for old age. They have to waste money buying in small quantities, and at wrong seasons, etc., because they haven't a large enough weekly margin to spend any considerable sum at once. The following is an example of this:

One time in summer when there was a big bankrupt sale of men's clothing, and various thrifty wives in comfortable circumstances were laying in supplies of winter clothes for husbands and children, I thought of a poor woman whose husband needed clothes badly, and was about to send her word of the sale. But suddenly I remembered that her husband was at that time making only $11.00 a week, and that she seldom had more than one dollar a week left, after paying for rent and gas and food for two adults and four children, and out of that $1.00 they were paying 50 cents a week on a bill at a furniture store, and there was always something needed even though most clothes for the family were donated. It seemed ironical that she should be told to go to a bargain sale! And such slight margins are typical. The tenement mother has to cast her mind's eye over the needs of her family and decide which child shall have the surplus each week, while extra trifles, like soap, thread, extra carfare, and especially shoes, are of staggering importance.

So that the very people who need to count every penny are the ones paying especially high prices for coal, flour, etc. They have to buy cheap food, which is not nourishing, and cheap ready-made clothes, which wear out quickly.

And yet people talk glibly of the " improvidence of the poor." Why, poor people can't even afford to buy things by the dozen. They simply pay the highest prices for the poorest foodstuffs. Indeed, considering their resources they manage wonderfully well, and of course occasionally do get unusual bargains.

People generally have no conception of the way the poor have to curtail expenditures; it is really pitiful, their efforts to make every cent tell. I remember once talking with a young widow, for whom I was ordering weekly groceries from a charitable association. She was telling me of her efforts to spread her supply of food, with supplements she was able to add, over the week. (She managed to pay rent and have a little over by doing washings.) She finally said, "And I never ask a neighbor in, even for tea and crackers, though it is hard not to be able to afford that much."

The whole subject of the difficulties of saving is summed up most succinctly by I. M. Rubinow in his book "Social Insurance." He says on p. 313:

"It is not necessary to repeat the general arguments made in an earlier chapter as to the absence of a continuous surplus from which savings could be made, as well as to the depressing effects of the saving habit on the standard of life. But we may point out, at this juncture, several reasons why the remedy of individual savings is even less applicable to the problem of old age than that of sickness or unemployment.

"I. The amount necessary is evidently greater, for old age is not a brief transitory condition, such as sickness or unemployment may be. It would require a continuous saving for a great many years.

"II. The amount necessary is uncertain. There is, after all, the even or more than even chance of early death before old age may be reached. And in addition, the wage-earner has no means at all to know how much he would have to save, nor whether his savings will prove sufficient.

"III. It is the final emergency, which in the natural course of events must be preceded by all other emergencies of a workingman's existence. Inevitably the fund of savings would have to be used to meet all these emergencies.

"IV. The remoteness of the emergency would prevent necessary savings at a time when such savings would be easiest, that is, in earliest years.

"V. To assume that under these conditions all workingmen could save sufficient to provide them against old age, would be to disregard all real conditions of the wage-worker's existence. Even in the most saving of our states, the average amounts held per depositor in the savings banks are ridiculously small as compared to the amount needed for a sufficient income at old age.

"VI. Finally, special saving for old age would only be possible through a persistent, systematic and obstinate disregard of the needs of the workingman's family, which would make the preaching of such special savings a decidedly immoral force."

X

EFFECTS OF DEPENDENCY OF THE AGED ON THEMSELVES, ON THEIR FAMILIES AND ON SOCIETY

WE have considered the causes of dependency of the aged and found many reasons and excuses for those who arrive at the age of about sixty years, and are unable to work, with no savings to live upon. We have also considered the position of the dependent aged, in several groups, but principally we have dwelt upon their incomes, and the incomes of those who support them, and upon the various other sources of maintenance.

I wish now to discuss and illustrate some of the effects of such dependency. My studies brought home to me not merely the tragedy of the dependency of the aged in its effects on themselves, but in its indirect effects. The old suffer, and even those who are uneducated, and undeveloped, and unused to the finer influences of life have instinctive, fine sensibilities, though their expressions of such sensibilities are most crude. Some of the cases I give in detail suggest the feelings of the aged, their dread of being burdens, etc. And often when they feel their children can support them fairly easily, they hate to give up and long to be independent. One poor old woman said to me (she was a cripple from doing laundry work), speaking of being supported by her unmarried son, a longshoreman, " If I could only make my own dollar again, instead of taking it from him, though he is kind! "

Some old people who still manage to work have not only themselves to provide for, but, with the link of the middle generation missing, have their grandchildren to provide for.

And still more pitiful are the old single people or childless couples, who feel that though they have contributed their share to the work of the world, they must accept charity at the end of their lives. They feel the bitterness of this.

Other families show that while the aged are slowly dying, the middle generation is being overworked and the young generation is being under-nourished.

This suggests that the middle generation has the burden of decision and responsibility as to the problem of the aged.

Formerly I supposed that many aged people were sent to institutions by families who would not support them, but I grew to realize that it was much oftener because they could not support them, judging by the efforts made by families to take the burden of support themselves.

Think of the middle generation trying to decide whether to support the aged parents and thus have less to eat for themselves and for their children, less for clothes, less room, and less for occasional recreation, or to put the old people in an institution!

One young married woman in Greenwich Village, whom I've mentioned before, told me that the time had come when her parents and her husband's parents all needed help. She said her husband's parents lived in New York in another district, and although the aged woman could still do a little work, i.e. washing and cleaning, she could not earn much, and the man couldn't earn anything. He was a shoemaker, but had such trembling hands he couldn't sew on shoes any longer, and anyway there wasn't much demand for hand-made shoes any more. The old man was looking for a job as a porter or watchman, but couldn't find a place. Her parents owned a little house with a garden in New Jersey and usually could "get along," but she had to send money to them occasionally, all that could be spared, for her husband earned only $12.00 a week. So she said, as his parents needed so much help, they would have to have outside aid, and she had, on advice, sent them to a charitable association for assistance.

Of course this is rather an unusual case, but it shows what can happen.

Another story was told me by a clergyman of one of the smaller churches in Greenwich Village. The clergyman expressed himself as much interested in the investigation and in the subject generally, but said he could not let me call on any of his people, fearing that my questions, however tactful, would in some way offend them, that even the poorest were hard-working, self-respecting and independent. He said, however, that he would tell me a story illustrating one phase of the effects of dependency of the aged. His story was in substance as follows:

An entirely worthy woman of ninety years, whose other relatives were all dead, lived with a married granddaughter. One night when she was awake she heard the granddaughter and her husband quarreling. The man said that he could not support the grandmother any longer; that he had his children to care for, and that any extra burden was intolerable. The young woman loved her grandmother and said she couldn't turn her out of the house. Next morning the old woman packed up her belongings and told her granddaughter that she had overheard the quarrel and that she could not be dependent on a man who felt her such a burden. The granddaughter remonstrated, but the grandmother was firm in her decision. She went to the clergyman, telling the story, and asked advice as to what to do. He happened to know of a charitable woman, then wealthy, who had risen from poverty, to whom he sent her. The charitable woman gave the poor old soul a definite pension, and sent her to board with some people in the country she knew, who took a few people, especially old people, to board. There in gratitude and comfort the old grandmother lived out her days. It was easier for her to take charity from a strange woman who could afford it, than from a connection who couldn't afford to support her and grudged her support.

So much for the effects on the old people themselves, and on the middle generation.

How does the dependency of the aged affect the grandchildren? To begin with, in families burdened by the support of the aged, or in families where there is a missing generation, the children have to go to work too early, or else there is the general lowering of standards at home. It is rather difficult to decide whether it is better for children to stay at school longer and be undernourished, or to go to work early and have more to eat, and yet this is a common problem for the poor to have to decide.

This problem came up not only in the cases I studied personally but in connection with families discussed by the settlement residents. Questions like these were heard: "Well, what had better be done—shall the grandmother or the child be placed in an institution? Can we tide Mrs. —— along till her grandson can work?" etc.! And this is illustrated also in cases Nos. 31 and 87 which are given a little farther on.

Before taking up the subject of the effect on the young people of going to work too early, I wish to speak of the family budget in general—that is, of the way it is made up. It is generally considered that a man's wages should support his family, and that only in cases of emergency should a woman whose husband is alive have to work. She is needed at home to care for the children and to do the cooking, washing, cleaning, etc. Let no one think that a tenement woman with, say, three children and a home to care for has much time for idleness. She can save much by giving proper attention to the buying and cooking of food and the making and mending of clothes. So needed is she in the home for the best interests of the children that those who have the administration of the widows' pension fund in the A. I. C. P. always arrange that the widows to whom the pension is given should do home work such as janitress work, etc., whenever possible. Nearly all educators, school truant officers, officers of the Gerry Society, and health officers agree that a mother with small children should be kept out of factories and at home.

But if the husband's wages are too small to support the family, and the wife cannot contribute to the budget, lodgers are often taken. But they are nearly always a detriment, as their presence means overcrowding and often is a serious moral menace to the family.

The only other solution for an inadequate budget is to send the children to work as early as possible. Several questions are involved here. When girls and boys go to work too early it is bad for their health, it is often dangerous for their morals, and it gives them in one way too much liberty, and in another way too great responsibility.

As soon as a girl or boy contributes to the family income, a feeling of independence develops, which is detrimental to parental authority. Economic independence heightens the sense of personal independence. At the same time this contribution, often of the entire wage earned except for money for carfare and luncheon and a few cents for spending money, sometimes makes the young people feel that an unfair burden falls on their shoulders. They work hard and yet gain little in food or clothing and almost nothing in added spending money.

There is often no time for the sons and daughters to go to trade schools. If the father is sick or out of work or dead, and especially if the family is laboring under the additional financial burden of an aged person, as soon as working papers can be secured the boys and girls are pushed into industry, and must have their entire industrial future ruined by lack of proper preparation, enduring meanwhile real hardships.

This is well brought out by Clara E. Laughlin in her book, "The Work-a-day Girl." Speaking of the Minimum Wage for Women, she says, on p. 166: "The average workingman . . . has probably been able to make no provision for these days of declining industrial worth which set in so comparatively early for him. When his daughter goes to work she should be able to relieve the strain by a little more than the cost of her keep; but she should be able to do it without those hardships of renunciation to which many of our young workers are driven by their parents' desperate desire to save against old age."

So the burden of the aged falls heavily upon the young.

The effects of the dependency of the aged upon society are of course very indirect, but are felt in the general lowering of wages, when the aged do try to work at lowest wages, and by the general lowering of family standards of living by the forcing of the young to work—which is not only bad for them, but also lowers wage standards and overcrowds industry. And by the overwork and overstrain of the middle and young generations the general physical efficiency is lowered, just as indeed all poverty with its accompanying undernourishment lowers the vitality and efficiency of the race.

The following cases serve as illustrations in part of these facts. Instead of the usual order of arrangement, —widows, single women, couples,—they are arranged as they illustrate effects on the old people, on the middle generation and on the grandchildren.

No. 95—Mr. T.

Mr. T., sixty-four years old, born in New York, has serious chronic indigestion; he looked really ill, and hasn't worked for one year. He and his wife live with a daughter separated from her husband, and a son of nineteen years. Of fifteen children there are eight left, and of all his sons the father said the youngest was the best, and the kindest to his parents. The father feels rather bitterly towards one son who could easily help him but won't. He resents his dependency deeply, especially as it falls on the youngest son. The daughter said, " Father always worked when he could." Mr. T. was a bricklayer and a truck-driver, earned $12.00 to $15.00 a week, but got down to $13.00 a week before he stopped work. He had no savings when he stopped work but a life insurance policy. However, his illness isn't the kind to end his life very soon necessarily, and he and his wife evidently are a burden and his feeling of uselessness and helplessness is pitiful.

No. 7—Mrs. D.

Mrs. D. illustrates a higher social grade than any of the others interviewed. She is well educated and refined and feels her position of dependency keenly. Her husband was well-to-do, but left her nothing. She was born in Ireland, but came to America when three years old, and is now over sixty. Never having worked any, she could do nothing to earn money after her husband's death but a little fine sewing. A wealthy friend gave her sewing to do, and gifts for years, but she finally died. Now Mrs. D. is living alone in a boarding-house, but said she might leave any time, but she would not go into an institution. Friends here and there help her out in a precarious way, and evidently she had appealed to a charitable association, as they gave me her name, saying she was a gentlewoman in need. She had apparently no church connection to help her. She was distressed and vague, and what is to become of her is hard to imagine.

No. 3—Mrs. B.

One can't help being sorry for Mrs. B., although she is rather an ungrateful old soul to the church which helps her, in addition to help from a settlement. She does suffer with fearful attacks of asthma, her struggles for breath are distressing to witness, but somehow one's sympathies go out especially to her daughter-in-law. This poor woman has to nurse her mother-in-law and go out doing cleaning, besides doing the janitress work where she lives (her husband, Mrs. B.'s son, being disabled and no financial help), and she is breaking down with all this work and overstrain.

No. 85—Mrs. P.

Mrs. P., an Italian woman of sixty-five, has been in New York twenty-seven years and can't speak English. Her daughter talked for her. The mother worked on a farm and sewed on trousers. Her husband died eight years ago, and sickness keeps her from working now, so she lives with her married daughters, who take her in turn. At present she is with a daughter who has six children. The young woman gave the impression that her mother was happy and took her dependency as a natural matter, and she said, " All of us daughters are willing to help mother, but our husbands are not, for they have their own mothers to help." The daughters all seem to need occasional outside help,—for example, milk at a milk station,—and once one of the daughters' husbands got a union card through a charitable society, and one daughter was sent to Sea Breeze. Evidently the families are on the border-line and every little extra counts.

No. 60—Mr. C.

Mr. C., an Irish widower of seventy-four years, seems to illustrate several effects of dependency. He worked in a factory, and then as a longshoreman, making $8.00 and $9.00 to $25.00 a week, i.e. getting these amounts irregularly—and finally made only about $2.50 a week before stopping two years ago, pushed out by younger men, naturally at seventy-two years of age. He had no savings when he stopped; even his insurance policy had run out. He lives with a son and his wife and five children. Two married daughters and some nephews evidently do not help. The daughter-in-law said her husband was a truck-driver making $15.00 a week, and with five children there wasn't much to spare, and she seemed to resent the support of her father-in-law, and he " wishes he had money of his own," so he is unhappy, and she is upset, and evidently all are cramped, and yet there is no one to blame for the situation.

It seems fair to give one example of real pauperism, though it is the only one I would call that, in the hundred investigated.

No. 28—Mrs. McC.

Mrs. Mc.C.'s family is not an example of the " worthy poor," but the reverse. The whole family illustrates the degenerating effects of extreme poverty.

Mrs. McC. herself at seventy can scarcely be blamed for not working, but she certainly has lost a great deal of her self-respect. She was born in Ireland and worked in a factory till she was married. Her husband was a weaver in Ireland, and came to the United States for "better wages," but succeeded in becoming only a day-laborer and died twenty-eight years ago. Then Mrs. McC. went out to do scrubbing and washing, and worked till three years ago. Then she had pneumonia and an abscess in her ear, and she is sick and feeble now. Of six children only two are left, and one cannot help, so she is dependent on a widowed daughter, with whom she lives. This daughter has four children, the youngest in a day nursery. The daughter works out by the day, but isn't successful, making only about $8.00 a month for the rent, and a little over. A charitable association provides some groceries. A church helps a little. Mrs. McC. confessed to the groceries, but said they did not have enough to eat, and rather begged for contributions. Afterward I found that several settlements had helped, sending the children away for vacations, etc., and that the mother was considered worthless. Now all these doles and makeshifts are bad for the family, especially the uncertainty of them, and the temptation is to rely upon them and to try for more aid instead of more work, for apparently the daughter could work more, and the effects are the worst upon her. Of course, old Mrs. McC. can't work, and it is possible to believe that the daughter worked hard years ago. The point of this story is meant to be that sometimes the strain for the middle generation is too great, and that occasionally people succumb, and that after all the individuals who fall are not always entirely to blame when conditions are too hard for them!

No. 31—Mr. M.

Mr. and Mrs. M. are separated, not through lack of affection, but because the only two of the eight sons and daughters living who can help their parents are two widowed daughters. One widowed daughter supports her father. She does janitress work, for which she gets nice light rooms and $10.00 a month. Then she does scrubbing at some offices, for which she gets

$20.00 a month. But $30.00 a month clear isn't much to feed two adults and two children and to clothe them and to provide for all emergencies. And she must work very hard to do the office and janitress work! She says her father doesn't realize what a burden he is. He worked on the docks for about $10.00 a week and when incapacitated hadn't saved anything. The old woman lives with the other widowed daughter. I just stumbled on this family when inquiring for someone else. I made two calls on the daughter with whom the old man lives, and one call at the house where the old woman lives—where I saw the old woman, but not the daughter. That daughter goes out cleaning and supports her mother and three children, and an invalid brother lives there too. The old woman gave the impression of living on very short rations and said, "I've just given the children some breakfast, but we didn't even have any sugar for the coffee." So apparently both families are struggling hard.

No. 87—Mrs. P.

The pastor of their church said, "You will find the S. family hard-working, self-respecting Germans," and I had known two of the boys slightly years before, in connection with some work in the neighborhood, as good and reliable. So I climbed the long stairs with expectations of a pleasant visit. I entered the kitchen and a comfortable scene met my eyes: a woman of about forty-five and one over sixty were sharing tea with a guest, another woman over sixty, whom I had heard of as a possible "case" for me. The boys served as an introductory theme, and then I was obliged to rest and have tea too—and to hear all the family news. While I recovered my breath, I learned that the family consisted of four generations, represented by one person from each generation. One of the boys and his little sister had died of tuberculosis, the boy recently, and now at last they understood about the disease, and had had the rooms well fumigated. The great-grandmother was in an adjoining room asleep; they said she was ninety and very feeble. The boy was at work. As I questioned more closely, from underneath this cheerful surface grim facts emerged. They said the boy didn't earn much yet of course, and not only his mother but the grandmother of sixty-three takes in washing,—both are widows. The boy's mother explained that they couldn't get enough washing to do and that was why "we seem so idle to-day." She would be glad if I could send more washing to them to do. The neighbor couldn't speak English very well, and was deaf, so I was told that they often gave bread and tea to her, as she had even less than they. Probably the great-grandmother won't live much longer, but by the time she dies the grandmother, now sixty-three, won't be able to do washing and help with expenses, and most unfortunately the mother isn't very strong, and the boy with his heritage and environment hasn't a very good prospect physically. I couldn't quite decide whom to pity most, the mother with the two older people to support and her fear for her last child's health, or the boy himself, who at the beginning of his working career is burdened with the three widows to assist. I felt that the boy, of course, was the one who might suffer most from the circumstances.

Thrift is here, and family devotion, and self-respect; they are too proud to receive financial aid from church or charity, but as all the boy's wages must go to his family, what has he for himself? And how overwhelming is the whole situation!

Some of these effects are well emphasized by I. M. Rubinow in his book "Social Insurance," on p. 315, when he says:

"But, nevertheless, there must be thousands of families where children are either unable or unwilling to render aid to the superannuated workers, but do it, nevertheless, because of deep attachment to the parents, or family pride revolting against application to charity, and that the filial obligation is thus enforced by a neglectful society with the effect of frequently depressing a standard of life already too low, or forcing the old father or mother to eat the daily bread unwillingly yielded, in pain and humiliation, or preventing the formation of a new family by the dutiful son or daughter because of the existing obligation towards the ruins of the old family."

And Alice W. Solenberger, in her book "One Thousand Homeless Men," says on p. 77, referring especially to men retired by industrial accidents: "When in such cases standards of living are lowered, and the earnings of children taken out of school must be resorted to, the indirect result will be revealed only in later years in the undermined vitality of these children. Yet this indirect result may be far more serious than the direct one."

XI

DISLIKE OF INSTITUTIONS

OF all the women I talked with only three thought they would like to go into an institution. One of a better position than most, evidently didn't like living with her brother and his wife, and just wanted to get away from them, and was perfectly vague about Homes; one lived alone and was scared by her attacks of dizziness, which sometimes caused her to fall and once caused quite an accident, and she was considering an offer from her church to put her in a Home. And the third, who was very lonely because of the recent death of her daughter, and didn't like living with her sister-in-law, although she was independent because she received a U. S. Army pension, thought also vaguely that she might like to go into a Home. But the overwhelming majority dreaded the very idea of an institution and fought bitterly against it.

At first I thought their fears were very unwarranted, just as their extreme fear of hospitals is. Though after visiting numerous free wards in hospitals one does realize that unless the poor patients are "interesting cases" they often are neglected, or are experimented with, and even when receiving proper attention they often do not understand what is happening to them; as one old woman I knew said, "They stuck needles into me, and I'm too old for needlework, and put me into a freezing box, when I'm so cold. I'd rather be in my own little basement, near the stove." Later, however, I found many of their fears about Homes substantiated. Even in the best of Homes there is a tremendous loss of liberty and individuality, and the inmates are at the mercy of the matron unless having "a pull" with some of the patronesses of the Home.

One gentlewoman I knew of was sent to the infirmary

in one of the very best Homes and was kept there five days before a doctor was summoned, and died as a result of neglect. Relatives then exerted themselves, an investigation was made, and forty-two complaints were received against the matron, who was finally dismissed.

Another gentlewoman, who had lost all her money, and all her friends, though her husband had been an editor and she had known distinguished people in her day, was placed by a church in one of the less well-known but supposedly satisfactory Homes. Most of the other inmates were foreigners, and they treated her very badly. She had a room with a woman who spoke no English, though there were other English-speaking inmates there. Some of the women actually "hazed" her, and stole food from her. The poor soul almost lost her mind under this treatment. Finally she was sent to a hospital to the psychopathic ward. When her church heard of this the doctors at the hospital were consulted, and as no mental derangement was found, except a certain loss of memory and vagueness natural to age though exaggerated by her trouble, she was removed from the hospital to a place outside of New York, where $1.00 a day board is paid for her and she is free and happy again, though many of her cherished belongings were lost at the first place.

It is only fair to add that I do know one or two very superior Homes for gentlefolk in reduced circumstances and that such Homes will always fill a certain need.

But if such things happen at high-grade institutions, think of the helplessness and sufferings of people placed in free institutions.

Men do not hate institutions quite as much as women. As I said in the chapter, "Aged People Wholly Dependent on Charity," men have not the same instinctive love of home-making and do not struggle as women, to keep a home, even if it is only a single room, with an oil-stove, which they use for heat and on which they prepare most meager meals.

Neither do men care quite as much for personal possessions and privacy, and they manage somehow even on

Blackwells Island to have more liberty than the women there, so they don't suffer the same when they " give up."

In order to see some of the actual conditions of those who gave up and went to public institutions for the aged, I visited the Home for the Aged on Blackwells Island and the Farm Colony on Staten Island. It is not necessary here to give descriptions of the two institutions in detail. I wish to mention merely what is particularly striking.

The Farm Colony is by far the superior, partly because of the cottage system and because married couples are not separated, and because it is smaller—with more ground, etc. There is one cottage containing sixteen couples, which is of course only a beginning in the right direction. And there are two other cottages there for women with single rooms, or rooms containing only two persons, and more cottages are to be built. Probably this system of cottages is more expensive and would not be practicable financially on Blackwells Island, but they might even on Blackwells Island have one big building for married people.

Many people who heard Albert Chevalier in his " Coster " songs, and were shocked at the revelation of the tragic separation of old married people in England, would be surprised to know that that system exists on Blackwells Island. But perhaps the most striking thing of all is the horror, of course greater because on a larger scale at Blackwells Island, of the huge dormitories with the beds nearer together than in the usual hospital wards. That people can sleep in such huge dormitories so close together seems incomprehensible—for although the very poor have never been used to the luxury of real privacy there is a difference between sharing a room with two to four relatives—and a room with a hundred or so strangers.

The hospital provisions at both places seem commendable and efforts are made for amusements, with occasional band concerts near the blind women's pavilion at Blackwells Island. And at Blackwells Island, under one of the churches, there is a library and reading-room where men and women both may go.

For sitting-rooms the men fare better at both places. There is no special enclosed gathering place for women at Blackwells Island, but the men have a big isolated one-room building which they call "Klondike," where they can smoke and play cards; at least I didn't see such a room for women, and we were guided around faithfully until in spite of long years of tenement visiting I could stand no longer the sight of such depressed, hopeless, sad, vacant, wretched faces. All seemed to live such a hopelessly monotonous life with no individuality or scope for personal effort.

And at Staten Island the men had a real sitting-room in the basement of one of the buildings; but the women had only their dining-room to use as a sitting-room, and it was much less comfortable and cheerful than the men's room, though women need homelike surroundings more than men.

The conclusion seems evident that men are given sitting-rooms at both places largely because of their smoking and chewing and spitting habits!

Of course people do get desperate and commit suicide or try to do so. One of the nurses at Blackwells Island said, "I don't think I can stand it here much longer, it is awful. I don't wonder some of the old people wander down to the river and get in boats and—well, sometimes nothing more is heard of them!"

At neither place did I have any opportunity to speak to any of the old people alone, but probably this was just chance, as of course visitors are allowed to come regularly to sing or read or talk with the inmates.

I feel I ought to say a word in commendation of the regulations for cleanliness, bathhouses, etc., at both places, and especially of the general hygienic regulations at Staten Island, where the disinfecting of clothes in the laundry, etc., is fine. With 3,000 people at Blackwells Island and 1,100 at the Farm Colony at Staten Island, cleanliness and hygiene are big problems.

My last comment is on the lack of provision at both places for the keeping of personal effects, which is a most serious defect.

At Staten Island, in the dormitories the women had

chairs by their bedsides, so they practically owned a chair as well as a bed, and the clothes on their backs. Think of the tragedy of owning nothing more, when every human being has inherently a love of acquisition of property, as is proved also in asylums for children, where it is found that children pine away if acquisition of personal belongings is denied them! I asked one of the heads at Staten Island if the inmates could not have a locked tin box for personal belongings, but he insisted that that would be a menace to the general hygiene. I said, "But the boxes could be inspected regularly." To which he objected irritably, "There is no one here to do such work. I am short of help as it is, besides the people here are riff-raff, anyway." This statement I could not agree with at all, for many of the inmates seemed very decent, respectable people, and in the cottages where they were given liberty (entrance to the cottages is rather by "pull," and perhaps to some especially deserving ones) they looked very neat and nice.

However, in all that has been said, I have tried not so much to criticize existing conditions at both places, as to criticize the whole system, for I hope some day other schemes for old-age provision will be found that will do away with such gigantic institutions.

Ideally, when possible, families should be "kept intact." As an important settlement worker said to me in effect, "The influence of the grandmother in the home of Italian families is very much needed. To begin with she often knows much more about the care of babies than the trained nurse or the mother. Secondly, her effect on the manners of the younger generation is important. She has more influence on the grandchildren than the mother has. And thirdly, besides the effect on manners, there is a deeper, more subtle influence that the grandparents exert. They inculcate reverence in the young, and moral steadiness. In the changing social and industrial conditions and the readjustments of racial habits of thought and life, though the young often lose respect for and obedience to their parents, somehow they still respect and obey their grandparents."

In a lesser degree this is no doubt true of other

nationalities. If grandparents could pay board to their families, when the families are too poor to support them, how much gain there would be doubly—to the aged and to their families.

Then there are the aged who have no families to board with, even if they had the money, but who, if they had the money outside that it must cost to keep them in an institution, could live alone or board with friends.

I cannot agree with F. Spencer Baldwin in this respect. He says in an article on "The Findings of the Massachusetts Commission on Old Age Pensions" in the American Statistical Association Publications for March, 1910: "The most interesting question that arises in connection with the almshouse population relates to the probable proportion of this class that would be enabled through the grant of pensions to withdraw from institutional residence. The facts as to the physical condition, earning power and family connections of inmates throw some light on this question. It appears that 93.8 per cent of the aged almshouse inmates have physical defects of some kind, and 79.1 are wholly incapacitated for labor, while an additional 8.4 are partly incapacitated. Thus the percentage of able-bodied in the aged pauper population is only 12.5. This fact points to the practical impossibility of removing any considerable portion of this population from the institutions through the establishment of a pension system. Another fact of similar significance is the extremely small percentage of almshouse inmates having adult children or other near relatives able to assist them, namely 7.7 per cent. It is obvious that aged inmates having no children or relatives with whom they could live would not, as a rule, be enabled by the grant of a small pension to leave the almshouse."

These statistics do prove that most people at the almshouses can't work to support themselves and that they are there because their relatives can't afford to support them, but it scarcely proves that their relatives or friends could not care for them if paid to do so; and plenty of these poor people in almshouses, even with physical disabilities, would prefer to live alone outside rather than stay in almshouses, if they had a little money which they could spend as they wished!

Now as to the cost of maintenance of the aged outside of institutions. It was practically impossible to calculate the cost of elderly people living with their families, but I gathered some data from people living alone.

Of women I found some existing on $3.00 a week, and one or two spending nearly $25.00 a month. Miss M., No. 25, in the chapter, "Aged People Wholly Dependent on Charity," had about $25.00 a month given her. Mrs. W., No. 48, in the chapter, "Aged People Who Are Self-Supporting," earned $6.00 a week. Mrs. N., No. 33, in the chapter, "Aged People Partly Self-Supporting and Partly Dependent on Charity," said she lived on $4.00 a week. Mrs. N., No. 84, in the chapter, "Aged People Supported Entirely by Their Families," said her son gave her $3.00 a week, and she "got along on that," and others managed on this amount. While Mrs. K., No. 75, in this chapter had really less than $3.00 a week.

Two people living together can get along on less, but couples at present are seldom supported outside of institutions, and where they are helped a little and earn something themselves it is difficult to ascertain their budgets. And elderly women, without relatives, insist on living alone, as far as my experience goes, so I have no data at all exact of two people living together.

Also I was unable to gather much data of men living alone from the men themselves, but some interesting information was given me at one of the Mills Hotels.

These Mills Hotels are not entirely philanthropic enterprises running at a financial loss, as is sometimes supposed, but pay, according to the statement of one of the clerks, a three and a half per cent dividend, which, of course, is not much of a return on the capital invested, but very far from a loss. There are about 4,000 men in the three Mills Hotels, with 1,554 rooms in the one I visited. One of the clerks there said that there were lots of men over sixty living there and working, and that their wages ranged from $5.00 to $25.00 a week.

The rooms are mostly twenty cents a night, and the meals are served à la carte, or table d'hôte at 15, 20 or 25 cents. Women are allowed in the restaurant only. There are large gathering rooms for the men, and all is not only clean but attractive too. Of course some men stop there who could afford to go elsewhere, but such men are not encouraged to stay.

It may be a perfectly impracticable suggestion, but if the State ever gives pensions of any kind, why couldn't the State then keep such hotels, and get back some of the money paid out? Then the State would be saved the expense of huge free institutions and the people themselves would be much better off.

To substantiate some of these remarks on the general dread of institutions, etc., the following is quoted from Alice W. Solenberger in her book, "One Thousand Homeless Men." On pp. 124 and 125 she says, "We found, too, that it was much more difficult to persuade persons to be financially responsible for the care of the old—particularly of old men—than it was of the young," and on pp. 126 and 127, "When in trying to secure adequate aid for self-respecting old men we found that there were neither relatives nor friends who could be interested in their behalf, and when because of breaking health the men were no longer able to work, we invariably were confronted with a problem which in most cases we were unable to solve because the lack of institutions made it impossible for us to offer the men the sort of care they should have had. As before stated, there were a few men whom we did not hesitate to send out to Dunning [the Chicago almshouse], and who were quite willing to go there, but of the twenty-five whom we finally placed in the poorhouse at least sixteen should have been cared for in some place where they could have been associated with a better class of men and where they would have been spared the unmerited stigma of shame which their residence in the poorhouse entailed," and on pp. 114 and 115 she quotes some entries made in records at the Bureau of Charities.

"Is tired and discouraged and says he is afraid he will have to give up and go to Dunning [the Chicago almshouse] soon," is an entry on one record. "Says he is physically well but mentally weary," is another.

"Is having a hard struggle. Is as strong as ever, but finds it increasingly hard to get work because he looks old." This from the record of a man of sixty who had lived forty years in Chicago and who had had good work records with a number of Chicago firms.

"Has had so little work this winter that he has almost starved, but cannot bear the thought of the poor-house."

"Unable to find any work. Says he is penniless, friendless and discouraged."

"Has no work yet, but says he would rather starve than go to Dunning."

"Such entries as these may be found on fifty per cent of the records of the old men applying to the Bureau, and these are not men who have been idle and profligate, but respectable Irish, German or American workmen, or, in some cases, business or professional men, many of whom have spent all their lives in Chicago, and have contributed their fair quota to its prosperity and wealth."

Here are a few descriptions of people taken from the hundred in this investigation.

No. 69—Mrs. D.

Mrs. D. was born in Brooklyn seventy-seven years ago. She said she left school at twelve "to help her mother." She never worked until after her husband's death and then she became a domestic nurse, making sometimes $10.00 to $12.00 a week. But four years ago she had to give up regular work, as she had heart trouble and wasn't strong, and she used up her savings in doctors' bills, etc. She never had children. She has a brother still older, but he can't help her. She lives alone in a furnished room, and is supported by odd jobs and gifts. She does not wish to go into a Home, but even if she did who would pay the usual entrance fee, for the church to which she belongs evidently can't do much for her, and it would be a shame to send her to a public institution.

No. 29—Mrs. McG.

Mrs. McG., over sixty, born in Philadelphia, was ill when I first visited her. She had a weak heart and had lost one eye. She told me she worked on passementerie before her marriage and after her husband's death. Some time ago she had a very serious illness, was taken to the hospital and the doctor told her she was not sick but starving, and that she must stay at the hospital for rest and nourishment. When she gained strength she went back to her two rooms, and someone in her church paid her rent—$8.00 a month—and she did church sewing for $1.50 to $2.00 a week, and had other gifts occasionally. Various people had tried to persuade her to go into a Home, but she absolutely refused to do so. Neighbors were kind, and she clung to her home and to being alone. She was not able to do the sewing when I first saw her, but expected to do it soon. When I saw her later she was better and quite cheerful. She thought the person who gave her the rent "very kind," but she felt that she really earned the money for the sewing, and she felt independent and loved her possessions and her own little kingdom. Later one of the nurses who went to see her found her dead—this the nurse had always prophesied would be the case. She probably died very suddenly and easily on account of her weak heart, or the neighbor across the way, who often helped her, would have been called in. Well, Mrs. McG. had what she wished, she kept her own home to the end!

No. 4—Mrs. B.

Mrs. B. was born in New York seventy-two years ago. She said she went to work at thirteen, "because of the panic." She has always made button-holes, at first as regular work, then as odd jobs, and now mostly for her church and two other societies, all of which contribute to her support. She lives alone and is still in good physical condition. She had the opportunity to be placed in one of the better-class Homes, one considered among the very best, but she refused to go. Some people consider her quite unreasonable; those who know most about even the best Homes sympathize with her!

No. 75—Mrs. K.

Mrs. K.'s name was given me by the wife of a pastor of one of the smallest churches in Greenwich Village. I found her living in a small tumbledown vacant house, in a small room, with her things overflowing into the hall. She has hardening of the arteries. She said her husband was a clerk and she never needed to work, but he drank heavily, and after his death, three years ago, there was nothing left but a very small insurance which lasted only a short time. Her sister-in-law in Washington gives her $5.00 a month and sometimes a little more, which pays for her wretched room, and for oil for a coal-oil stove, and her church and her friends provide food. She said a charitable society had helped her formerly, but refused at present to help. She said the society tried to get her into a Home, but she refused to go. The society, when I communicated with them, insisted that her sister probably helped her more than she admitted, and that anyway she should be forced into a Home, as she was too sick to live alone and had such a dirty room that it was a menace. I agreed that her room was dirty, but I had seen others just as dirty from which tenants were not forced to move, and as the woman can't live long (she wishes herself to die soon), it did seem as if food and an occasional "cleaning-up" might be provided for her and she might be left in peace.

No. 70—Mr. G.

Mr. and Mrs. G. live on Jones Street, and almost every time I passed by the house in which they live I saw Mr. G. stationed on the front steps where he could watch all the numerous activities of the street, and always received a cheery greeting. He can hobble around a little, but can't work since he was paralyzed five years ago. He was paralyzed on one side, and is blind in one eye. He was born in New York City sixty years ago, and according to the investigations of one of the charitable societies had a good record and received good testimonials from his employers. He told me that as a boy he worked with a clothing company, and then did trucking and later was a butcher, making at his highest success $1,000 a year. Then he was in a United States Appraiser's store, where he earned $70.00 a month, and finally he was a keeper on Blackwells Island, where he got $60.00 to $70.00 a month. When he could no longer work he had some savings, but those are exhausted now, though he still manages to keep up his insurance policy payments. His wife goes out washing and cleaning, but doesn't make enough to support both of them, and they refuse emphatically to go to an institution! As he said to me, "I know what Blackwells Island is like!" A brother and two stepdaughters can't help. Old employers and the State National Guard, to which Mr. G. belonged, have been appealed to, but as yet not with satisfactory results. At present Greenwich House and the C. O. S. help them a little, and a scheme is on foot to raise some sort of regular allowance from various sources.

XII

THE NEED OF PUBLIC PROVISION FOR AGED PEOPLE IN AMERICA

NOW, certainly the close study of even the hundred people in this investigation leads to the belief that there are old people unavoidably dependent, because they cannot work, and that their families cannot, or will not, or ought not to support them, and that putting people into big institutions is not a satisfactory way of solving the old-age problem,—in short, that some other provision for dependent old people should be made.

This provision for old age is usually made in Europe by some sort of social-insurance or pension system.

It is not within the province of this report to discuss: (1) the different schemes of pensions or social insurance in any great detail, or to point definitely to which is the best and wisest to institute in America, or (2) the number of people who would be eligible for such provision, or (3) the cost of such provision,—an attempt has been made merely to add to the evidence on the subject of the actual need for provision for the aged, not merely for their own sakes, but for the sake of their families and even for the sake of society.

The subject of pension and social-insurance systems is growing in importance. One writer sums up the kinds of pension and insurance systems as follow: (1) Voluntary Private Old-Age Insurance; (2) Subsidized Voluntary State Insurance Against Old Age; (3) Compulsory Old-Age Insurance; (4) Non-Contributory Old-Age Pensions; and these are thoroughly described in the books mentioned in Chapter I.

All these systems are being tried in various countries, and America is at last seriously considering the problem. I. M. Rubinow says in his book on Social Insurance (p.

411): "The demand for an old-age pension has for over twenty years constituted a permanent plank in the platform of the Socialist Party, but for the first time it has now become a living issue, as is proven by the fact that it has been included in the famous 'confession of faith' and in the National and New York State platforms of the Progressive Party."

And certain states have taken preliminary steps in the same direction. So it is to be hoped that the way will be found by which provision for the aged can be made, adequately and acceptably, and yet with less expense than is often feared!

To stop generalizing and to return to the scope of this particular investigation, it was most surprising to realize the difficulty with which I found one hundred aged people suitable for this study in the large area of Greenwich Village. Of course, this is only a drop in the bucket by way of evidence, but it seems to me a rather significant drop. There are probably not as many aged people needing state provision as is often feared. But those who need provision need it badly. The present provisions are not only pitifully inadequate but exceedingly hit-or-miss—much too much is left to chance.

I hope I have indicated clearly the fear of institutions which hangs over the poor, and the generally merited dislike for them. Institutions are not a satisfactory mode of provision for the aged, and could never be made so.

Secondly, although many churches make efforts to help their aged members they seldom have funds enough to help very many, and besides dependent aged people who are church members form a very small group, i.e. members of Protestant churches; and Roman Catholic churches give comparatively little financial aid. It was interesting to see that the people really belonging to churches and helped by their churches seemed on the whole more self-respecting than those helped by charity, i.e. charitable societies.

Thirdly, the charitable agencies, with all their laudable efforts, are not able to cope with the situation of providing adequately for aged people outside of institutions. As one agent of a society said to me: "We can raise only small funds for assisting aged people outside of institutions. The public is asked to support institutions and naturally expects the dependent aged to be put into those institutions." And not only do the charitable societies not have funds enough to provide for the aged, but their assistance, except in sharp emergencies, has unfortunately a deteriorating effect upon the recipients. I heard of one young married woman, whose family in her childhood had been regularly assisted by charity, who said, "Rather than have my children supported by charity I'd kill them all." It seems as if the whole attitude of large charitable societies had to be, under present conditions, much too high-handed.

In a collection of stories entitled "Mrs. Mahoney of the Tenements," by Louise Montgomery, there is a story, "Case No. 1199," of a charity visitor who has an old man moved to a hospital without his or his wife's consent. The neighbors take up a subscription, and one young man goes to the hospital, and, claiming to be the son, takes the old man home to die, as the doctor admits he probably won't live for a month. Now this story probably has no basis in actual facts. As powerful as the charitable societies are, they are not allowed, even if they wished, to remove patients to hospitals by force—only the Board of Health is allowed to do that, when the patient is considered a menace to the family and the neighborhood. But the story does illustrate a certain attitude of charitable societies and of many people, rich or well-to-do, towards the poor, and this is the attitude, in a blunt form—"If we help you even partly as well as wholly, you must do as we direct absolutely." Now, it seems to me that this is, not always but often, an unreasonable and exceedingly high-handed attitude. It is the attitude of power towards the defenceless, and it seems only justice that the state shall guard all its citizens in such a way that they shall never reach the point where their destinies are so dominated. And besides, think of the towns and villages where there are no organized charities!

Nor does it seem that, in a true democracy, provision for citizens of any class should be left to another class to be given as charity. When people have contributed all their lives to the industry of their state, should they be obliged at the end of their days to depend on charity? After struggling to keep their self-respect by hard work all their lives, think of the choice at the end, to go to an institution, or else to deprive their families of the very necessities of life!

The people who receive United States war pensions do not feel so disgraced, and I was much interested in the attitude of the people I saw one morning at the " Exempt Firemen's Association " rooms. The women sitting waiting for their pensions looked respectable and self-respecting. I fell into conversation with one of them, and she explained, " Our husbands belonged to the volunteer firemen in the old days, you know, and now we are just being paid back dues; it isn't a charity pension, you see! " This idea of " justice " rather than " charity " is well brought out by F. W. Lewis, in his book, " State Insurance," when he says on p. 150: " In the more recent discussions of old-age relief we hear more of doing justice and less of bestowing charity. The preamble to the old-age pension act in New Zealand recites that it is equitable that those who, in the prime of life, helped to bear the public burdens of the Colony and to open up its resources should receive pensions, and in the debate in the British Parliament upon the recent old-age pension act, the Chancellor of the Exchequer said, in reply to the demand for a contributory plan: 'The workman who has contributed health, strength, vigor and skill to the building-up of the wealth of the nation has made his contribution.' "

And the constructive side of social provision for old age is brought out in the following quotations. I. M. Rubinow says in his book " Social Insurance " (p. 312): " But the purpose of a social policy in dealing with destitution is not only to substitute for private and public charity, is not only to prevent starvation, not only, in short, to prevent the extreme of pauperism, but also to cure or prevent poverty, to prevent semi-starvation, to raise conditions of life, standards of life for the victims as well as for the working-class as a whole, by removing the depressing effect upon wages and the standards of living which a large contingent of pauperized or semi-pauperized or simply destitute individuals must necessarily exercise." And Henry R. Seager says in his book "Social Insurance" (p. 118): "The proper method of safeguarding old age is clearly through some plan of insurance. Old age is a risk to which all are liable, but which many never live to experience. Thus, according to American life tables, nearly two-thirds of those who survive the age of ten die before the age of seventy. Under these circumstances, for every wage-earner to attempt to save enough by himself to provide for his old age is needlessly costly. The intelligent course is for him to combine with other wage-earners to accumulate a common fund out of which old-age annuities may be paid to those who live long enough to need them."

So far the authors quoted have been in favor of some system of social insurance, or of pensions—the majority advocating the former. Let us now turn to objections given to pensions, and to some discussions on voluntary and compulsory insurance.

There seems to be rather a good deal of fear that state pensions would injure the "self-respect of the workingman" and "discourage thrift" and have a "disintegrating effect on families."

In the *American Labor Legislation Review* for June, 1913, in an article on "Old-Age Insurance," F. Spencer Baldwin, Secretary of the Massachusetts Commission on Old-Age Pensions, says (p. 210): "The thrift habit is not something instinctive and spontaneous; it is the race product of careful training. It is extremely hard to build up and very easy to break down. The aim of modern poor-law reform has been to cultivate this habit by penalizing unthrift and stigmatizing dependency. The establishment of the pension system means the abandonment of this approved policy of conserving thrift, and reversion to the discredited methods of general outdoor relief. The gravest consequences are to be apprehended from the new policy. In general it must exert an enervating and demoralizing influence on character, lessening the sense of personal responsibility, self-reliance and self-respect, and sapping the foundations of individual independence, initiative and resourcefulness.

"Finally, the effect of non-contributory pensions on the family must be set down as a further objection to the plan. A non-contributory pension system weakens the bonds of family solidarity. It takes away in part the filial obligation for the support of aged parents, which is one of the main ties that hold the family together. The supporters of the pension policy deny that this result would follow. They contend that, on the contrary, their plan would strengthen the family; they reason that the payment of small pensions to old people would help to keep families together by making it possible for the children to retain the aged parent in the household, in view of the addition that his pension would bring to the family income. While this might be true in individual cases, it can hardly be doubted that the general effect on the family would be disintegrating. The assumption by the state of the obligation to support the aged in their homes would undermine filial responsibility precisely as the guarantee of public maintenance of children would destroy parental responsibility. The impairment of family integrity is, in fact, one of the most serious dangers threatened by recent experiments with non-contributory pensions."

And the same author says in the American Statistical Association Publications of March, 1910, in an article entitled "The Findings of the Massachusetts Commission on Old-Age Pensions" (p. 18): "A non-contributory pension system is simply a counsel of despair. If such a scheme be defensible or excusable in this country, then the whole economic and social system is a failure. The adoption of such a policy would be a confession of its breakdown. To contend that it is necessary to take this course is to assume that the members of the working-class either cannot earn enough or cannot save enough to take care of themselves in old age. If that be true, then American democracy is in a state of decay which no system of public doles could possibly arrest, but would rather hasten."

Now, it seems to me that the small benefit given

by a pension at the end of life would scarcely encourage men to be reckless in earlier years. And as I have tried to demonstrate from practical instances in the chapter, "Difficulties of Saving for Old Age," much saving for old age is impossible. Thrift is needed for wise expenditures and proper living, and is scarcely possible as productive of saving for old age. And surely families would not love their aged members less if they were not such financial burdens, but more. And of course no one would consider that pensions are a remedy for low wages—they are merely palliatives while wages are low. One might with equal accuracy say that we should not have hospitals for tuberculosis, as it is a preventable disease, though no one doubts the need of hospitals till the disease is entirely eradicated!

And there seems to be great fear that the poor will not have enough opportunity for self-sacrifice!

Frederick L. Hoffman says in the American Statistical Association Publications for March, 1909, on p. 367: "A non-contributory old-age pension scheme will not solve the problem of the dependent poor and will not prevent an increase in the burden of real pauperism; but, on the contrary, it will undermine and tend to destroy the self-respecting character of our people as citizens in a democracy where economic independence, achieved by individual effort, self-sacrifice, and self-denial, is, after all, the only aim and end worth while."

Surely the poor when known individually have plenty of exercise for these virtues of self-denial; it could not harm them to remove a few of their difficulties. My own appreciation of the futility of these arguments found confirmation in the comments on them by I. M. Rubinow in his book so often referred to, "Social Insurance." On pp. 314 and 315 he gives first a quotation from the report of the Massachusetts Commission on Old-Age Pensions:

"'*The disintegrating effect on the family.* A non-contributory system would take away, in part, the filial obligation for the support of aged parents which is the main bond of family solidarity. It would strike at one of the forces that have created the self-supporting, self-respecting American family. The impairment of family solidarity is one of the most serious consequences to be apprehended.'" And then he says: "There is a good, old-fashioned atavistic nobility of sentiment about this argument which will greatly please all good men and women except those who have to be supported by their children, and those who have to support their parents and also their own families on a wage-earner's budget. . . . It further seems to assume that we love our burdens and that when parents cease being burdens the children cease loving them. It assumes that the standing of a superannuated parent in a family is in an inverse proportion to the amount he is able to contribute to the family budget. It is an appeal to an ideal of a patriarchal family which has been dead for a century in every industrial country, and which really never had any strong hold upon American life. Of course, its inapplicability to the aged single man or the aged spinster aunt will be evident. For it certainly cannot be claimed that the support of all spinster aunts is also a fundamental principle of American solidarity. Then again, even married people may not have any children, or may have lost them. . . ." And he says much more of interest on this subject, not in praise of a pension system, but to prove that these particular arguments against pensions are not valid and to urge the need of some sort of social provision.

Another question is brought up in these articles—the difference between pensions given to civil employees and war veterans and to workingmen in general. In his article, "State Pensions and Annuities in Old Age," in the American Statistical Association Publications for March, 1909, Frederick L. Hoffman says on pp. 368 and 369: "The argument is advanced that such pensions are really not fundamentally different from the pensions paid to soldiers and sailors for service rendered the nation in times of peace or war, or to civil service employees of all kinds, who are retired on attaining a given age; for it is said, if the state considers it just to pension our fighters, why should she not also pension workers? . . . The case is very different with men who have followed their own ends and served their own purposes, who have made their struggle for success and who, because of misapplied energy or misapplied talent or because most likely of misspent years, are dependent upon charity in their old age. The more than thirty millions of men and women employed in the industries of this country are not working for the state or for the nation, but they are working for themselves, and they have unrestrained control over the expenditures of their incomes, and, to that extent, they have their future fate in their hands. These are the workers of the nation, but not the workers for the nation, and the difference is fundamental, and ought never to be lost sight of in discussions of this kind."

Isn't this rather more theoretic than actual, all this about "misspent years" and "unrestrained control over expenditures"—and how can soldiers be considered such unselfish laborers for the nation?—they surely are quite as self-seeking as factory workers, for example.

Besides, if pensions are so fearfully demoralizing, why are private pension systems so lauded? In an article entitled "The Work of the Massachusetts Commission on Old-Age Pensions," in the American Statistical Association Publications for March, 1909, F. Spencer Baldwin says, on p. 426, referring to private pension schemes: "The general nature of the leading schemes is substantially the same. Provision is made for the voluntary or compulsory retirement of employees at a certain age, with weekly or monthly allowances. The amount of the allowance is determined by the length of service and the wages of the employee. It is usually calculated on a basis of a percentage of the average wages for each year of service. The expenses of the pension system are commonly borne by the employer without contribution from the employee. Often the pension system is combined with provision for sickness and accident insurance organized on a contributory basis. The motives that have induced large corporate employers to provide retirement pensions are partly economic and partly humanitarian or philanthropic. Economic motives play the leading part. This thing has been done because it has been found to be good business policy. The economic gain from the pension system is twofold: it eliminates the waste and demoralization attendant upon the continued employment of old men who have outlived their usefulness, and it helps to promote industry, contentment, and loyalty on the part of the working force. The pension system aids in solving the difficult problem of stimulating the employees of a large corporation to the highest efficiency," etc.

Why are public pensions so much more harmful than pensions given by corporations?

Having given these arguments for and against the pension system, it seems only fair to give a few arguments for and against insurance schemes.

In an article by F. Spencer Baldwin, "Old-Age Insurance," in the *American Labor Legislation Review* of June, 1913, he says, on p. 206, speaking of the Massachusetts savings-bank insurance system: "The weakness of the plan is the fundamental failing of all voluntary insurance systems, it fails to reach the mass of the working population, especially the class of low-paid laborers most in need of some provision for old age. As Professor Schaeffler has well said: 'Experience has everywhere demonstrated that the great mass of those workingmen who are poorly off will not voluntarily insure themselves. Furthermore, the great majority of those who would like to do so cannot on account of the smallness of their earnings. In other words, it is exactly that class which is most in need of insurance that either will not or cannot avail themselves of this device.' The statistics of the savings-bank insurance in Massachusetts show that very little use has been made of the provisions for the purchase of annuities." A most interesting article on the Massachusetts Savings-Bank Insurance and Pension System is that by Louis D. Brandeis in the American Statistical Association Publications for March, 1909.

From my own little experience also I can see that very few are able to pay for voluntary insurance. Whenever possible, the poor keep up their "burial insurance," as fear of a pauper's grave is one of their most pressing and terrifying anxieties, but often they are unable to keep up even the small payments demanded for that insurance.

To be sure, in late years the whole system of private insurance has improved greatly, and it might be improved still more, so that life insurance would cost the poor less and give them greater benefits. But no system of private life insurance or the payment of annuities could ever solve the problem of providing adequately for old age, for it would provide only for the better-paid class of working-people, not for those who need such provision most.

Now, if the very poor can't pay for voluntary insurance, how could they pay for compulsory insurance, even if that insurance were contributed to by the state and by employers also? On p. 19 of the American Statistical Association Publications for March, 1910, F. Spencer Baldwin says in the article before referred to on "The Findings of the Massachusetts Commission on Old-Age Pensions": "It may be that eventually the state will undertake to enforce this obligation upon the individual by law. The state may, in the interest of all, say to the individual: 'You shall provide for your old age through saving made easy by a system of insurance established by government, in order that the general welfare may not be disturbed by your coming to the state for support in your old age.' The principle of compulsory education has been adopted and widely extended. The principle of compulsory sanitation has been applied in various directions. The principle of compulsory insurance might be defended as a needful measure of further state interference for the protection of society against the burden of old-age pauperism, precisely as compulsory education and compulsory sanitation have been instituted to protect society against ignorance and disease. A system of state insurance thus grounded, however, would be based on the principle of enforced obligation on the part of the individual to insure himself and not on that of recognized duty on the part of the state to pension all worthy citizens. The British and Australian pension systems are based on the latter principle, involving the doctrine that a citizen may claim a pension from the state as a civil right. That doctrine is distinctly un-American. The opposite principle of obligatory insurance, as here interpreted, is the only one that could possibly be harmonized with American conditions, traditions and ideals."

Now it seems to me that compulsory education and sanitation, and compulsory insurance are scarcely parallels, for the burden of their payment falls very differently. And also it seems to me that however individualistic our early American methods may have been, we are at last working out ideas of more co-operative responsibility. As Henry R. Seager says in his book "Social Insurance" (p. 19): "The failure of wage-earners to provide, each for himself, against the contingencies that I have specified—accidents, illness, premature death, unemployment and old age—is to my mind merely proof that collective remedies must be found and applied to these evils."

So far no one system of provision for old age seems entirely satisfactory; all pension systems and all insurance systems seem to fail in some respects. But perhaps some combination or modification of these systems will be discovered. It scarcely seems to me that the workers could contribute much money towards any system themselves, but perhaps those receiving over a certain wage might, and perhaps not only all manufacturers but all employers might contribute, and the state might levy some tax for the fund, and then pensions could be graded as to amounts given, with certain qualifications (as was first proposed in England), and this might be administered with less cost than some writers fear, through post offices or banks or municipal employment bureaus, or even municipal co-operative workshops! Surely some provision for the aged ought to be made and will be made in time.

The general situation is well summed up by I. M. Rubinow in his "Social Insurance" (pp. 42 and 43): "To sum up: (1) From two-thirds to three-fourths of all productive workers in the United States depend upon wages or small salaries for their existence. (2) From four-fifths to nine-tenths of the wage-workers receive wages which are insufficient to meet the cost of a normal standard of health and efficiency for a family, and about one-half receive very much less than that. (3) If a certain proportion of wage-workers' families succeed in attaining such a standard, it is made possible only by the presence of more than one worker in the family. (4) This condition, however, can only be temporary in the history of any workingman's family. (5) The increase in the standard of wages is barely sufficient to meet the increased cost of living. (6) An annual surplus in the workingman's budget is a very rare thing, and is very small. (7) The growth of savings-bank deposits in the United States is not sufficient evidence of the ability of the American workingmen to make substantial savings. A large proportion of these savings belong to other classes of population, and in so far as information is available the average workingman's deposit is very small. (8) The analysis of the economic status of the American wage-worker does not disclose his ability to cope with the various economic emergencies without outside assistance."

Formerly people thought that the working-people in America were as a whole so much better off than the working-people abroad that no special provision need be made for the aged in America. These optimistic beliefs, however, have been somewhat shattered.

But to return to the evidence in this particular investigation. Surely some of the cases described in the preceding chapters point to the fact that many old people suffer greatly, mentally and physically, and that no existing provisions fit their needs. Only those who really know and respect the hard-working, independent poor realize their struggles, their sensitiveness and their heroism against overwhelming odds.

Should we not encourage wage-earners to keep up their standards of living throughout their lives, and when their wage-earning power is over, if it is necessary for their sakes and for the sake of their families to help, shall we not provide them with the opportunity to live with independence and self-respect in their old age?

www.ingramcontent.com/pod-product-compliance
Lightning Source LLC
LaVergne TN
LVHW021431110826
845150LV00007B/2179

* 9 7 8 1 4 2 5 5 0 7 7 7 0 *